AF590941

CONTENTS

INTRODUCTION

Most people agree that breakfast isn't the same without bread in it. The type, form, color, or quantity does not matter. Everyone simply wants some bread! The Cuisinart Convection Bread Maker is a beautifully and delicately constructed machine with 680 watts power output and a convection fan, an authentication of its speed and effectiveness.

With sixteen menu options, most of your baked favorite's bases are covered. Also, the unique gluten-free function sets this convection bread maker apart from others. This feature promises a healthy baked result.

The Cuisinart Convection Bread Maker cookbook informs you of many wonderful baked foods you can make with the Cuisinart Convection Bread Maker in little time and in the confines of your home.

Enjoy!

CHAPTER 1: FUNDAMENTALS OF CUISINART CONVECTION BREAD MAKER

What is the Cuisinart Convection Bread maker

The Cuisinart Convection Bread Maker is a brushed stainless steel cooking machine designed to transform your baking game. It is cuboid-like and comprises a *stainless steel lid with a glass viewing window, a control panel, an LCD, a baking chamber with two side handles, a power cord, and a heating element.* Other essential accessories include a *detachable baking pan with a handle, kneading paddle, measuring cup, and measuring spoon.*

Furthermore, it operates with *sixteen preset cooking programs, a hundred plus baked food choices* (bread, pizza dough, cake, etc.), *three crust color options* (light, medium & dark), and *three loaf size options* (1, 1.5 & 2 pounds) to produce magnificent results.

Amazingly, this is not the end of all the wonderful features that make up the Cuisinart Convection Bread Maker. Check out more detailed points in the next section.

The benefits of using the various functions of the Cuisinart Convection Bread Maker

Here are the benefits accrued to you as you utilize your Cuisinart Convection, Bread Maker.

- **BPA (bisphenol A.) free components:** BPA is a chemical commonly used by manufacturers to make plastics and coat the interior of some metallic products. This chemical is very harmful to health. Fortuitously, the components/accessories of the Cuisinart Convection Bread Maker are BPA free. Therefore, you safe from negative health effects.
- **Low carb/gluten-free function:** Quite a number of us are often concerned about the fat/carb/glutton contents of what we eat. With this wonderful feature, you can bake without any health worries.
- **Audible alerts:** These are sound signals to alert you about certain operations of the bread maker. They are;

1. **The Mix-ins signal** occurs fourteen minutes before the completion of the second knead. It contains four sets of five long beeps each.

2. **The End bake signal** indicates that the bake cycle is over with ten beeps. Twelve beeps signal the end of the keep warm cycle.

Note: This function activates right after the bake cycle is over, and it holds for sixty minutes.

3. **The Remove paddle signal** occurs a little before the last rise-cycle. It contains three sets of six beeps each to remind you to withdraw the kneading paddle.

4. **The Jam cycle signal** alerts you to scrape the baking pan's interior at a five to ten minutes interval. Remember to use a nonstick spatula.

5. **The error beep** to indicate you have pressed a wrong function.

- **Sixteen cooking presets:** This gives you many options, all you have to do is choose. These are the presets in no particular order: French/Italian, rapid French/Italian, rapid white, white, rapid whole wheat, whole wheat, sweet bread, rapid sweet bread, Quick bread/cake, Artisan dough, last-minute loaf, dough/pizza dough, jam, gluten-free, low carb, and bake only.
- **The Pause function and the Power failure reinforcement**
- **Easy to get replacement parts:** Detachable parts such as the baking pan, measuring spoon and cup, and Kneading paddle are easy to replace in the event of damage by contacting Cuisinart to make an order.

Tips for Best use of the Appliance

- Make use of precise measurements of the ingredients or follow the recipe's stipulations judiciously to avoid unsatisfactory outcomes.
- Ingredients must be arranged inside the baking pan in the correct order; the fluids (water, milk, etc.) first, then the dry ingredients (flour), and the yeast/baking powder.
- Brush kneading paddle lightly with vegetable oil for easy withdrawal if stuck in the loaf.
- When using a bread-baking machine, your location's temperature and humidity affect the dough's consistency, negatively affecting the result. To avoid this, weigh the flour with a kitchen scale before use, and add the other ingredients with a teaspoon at intervals as required. Add flour when the dough is too wet and water when it is too dry.
- Do not use the delay start function while using perishable ingredients like milk, eggs, fruits, and vegetables.

- Study the user manual before to avoid accidents and avoidable mistakes.

How to Clean and Maintain the Cuisinart Convection Bread Maker

- Before first use, clean the unit thoroughly.
- After every use, remove the baking pan and kneading paddle. Wash in a dishwasher or by hand with a soft sponge and soapy water. Rinse and dry with a clean towel.
- Use a damp cloth/sponge to clean the baking chamber and then dry thoroughly before the next use.
- Furthermore, wipe the bread maker's exterior, the lid, and the control panel with a damp rag. Never immerse these components in water or any other fluid.

Troubleshooting for the Appliance

- **Why is the bread maker making these strange noises?** This is because the bread pan has not properly snapped into place, resulting in the collision of the bread pan and the baking chamber's interior. The ingredients will also not knead properly. Follow the manual's instructions when positioning the bread pan.
- **Why is the bread maker smoking and emitting a burning smell?** This usually occurs when ingredients have spilled into the cooking chamber. Firstly, unplug the unit, use an oven mitt to lift the bread pan out, and carefully clean the spillage. Replace the pan afterward and resume the cook cycle. This is all possible because of the 15 minutes program memory of the bread maker.

CHAPTER 2: CLASSICAL BREAD

Simple Sandwich Bread

Simple sandwich bread is basic for other bread recipes. It is delicious and easy to bake with the Cuisinart bread maker

Prep time: 5 minutes

Cooking time: 3 hours 25 minutes

Serves: 1 Loaf

Ingredients To Use:

Dry ingredients

- 3 cups of flour
- 2 tbsp. active dry yeast
- ¼ cup of granulated sugar
- 2 tsp xanthan gum
- 1 tbsp. baking powder
- 1 tsp kosher salt
- 1 /8 tsp ascorbic acid

WET INGREDIENTS

- 1 cup of plus 2 tbsp. of water heated to 80°F
- 3 large eggs at room temperature
- ¼ cup of olive oil
- 2 tsp. apple cider vinegar

Step-by-Step Directions to Cook It:

1. add olive oil, vinegar, and water in a bowl; combine until well incorporated.
2. Break the egg in a bowl and whisk; add the olive oil mixture and set aside.
3. Add the yeast in a small bowl and set aside; add flour, xanthan, salt, baking powder, ascorbic acid in a bowl and mix
4. Pour the liquid ingredients into the Cuisinart bread pan, then spread the Dry ingredients on top
5. Make a shallow well in the center and add the yeast
6. insert Cuisinart bread pan back to the Cuisinart Bread Machine
7. Close the lid and Select the program; White
8. Select medium crust color and loaf size; 1 ½-lb. press the start button
9. Remove bread and allow to cool; serve, and enjoy.

Serving Suggestion:

Preparation and Cooking Tips: leave the bread to cool before serving

Nutritional value per serving: Calories: 123kcal, Fat: 5g, Carb: 24g, Proteins: 9g

Tender Buttermilk Bread

The tender milk is a beautiful and soft cream-colored bread that is delicious. It has a tangy flavor that you will love

Prep time: 5 minutes

Cooking time: 3 hours 25 minutes

Serves: 1 Loaf

Ingredients To Use:

Dry ingredients

- 3 cups of Light Flour Blend
- 1 tbsp baking powder
- 2 tbsp. active dry yeast
- ½ cup of buttermilk powder
- 3 tbsp. granulated sugar
- 2 tsp xanthan gum
- 2 tsp kosher or fine salt
- 1/8 tsp ascorbic acid

WET INGREDIENTS

- 1 tsp apple cider vinegar
- 3 large eggs, whisked
- 4 tbsp. unsalted butter (melted and cooled)
- 1 cup of plus 2 tbsp. water warmed to 80°F (27°C)

Step-by-Step Directions to Cook It:

1. Add butter, vinegar, eggs, water, and mix
2. Add the yeast to a bowl and set aside.
3. Add the dry ingredients to another bowl and mix
4. Pour the liquid ingredients into the Cuisinart bread pan, then spread the Dry ingredients over it
5. Make a well in the mixture and add the yeast.
6. insert Cuisinart bread pan back to the Cuisinart Bread Machine
7. Close the lid and Select program; white.
8. Select Crust color; medium and Loaf size; 1 ½-lb. press the start button
9. Remove bread and allow to cool; serve, and enjoy.

Serving Suggestion: Toast with grilled cheese

Preparation and Cooking Tips: make sure ingredients is at room temperature

Nutritional value per serving: Calories: 241kcal, Fat: 5g, Carb: 27g, Proteins: 12g

Brioche Loaf

The brioche loaf is a buttery, rich, and delicious bread that is perfect for dinner. It can be used in the preparation of toast.

Prep time: 5 minutes
Cooking time: 3hours 25 minutes
Serves: 1 Loaf

Ingredients To Use:

DRY INGREDIENTS

- 4 cups of bread flour
- 1/3 cup of granulated sugar
- 2 tsp active dry yeast
- ¼ cup of milk powder
- 1 tsp xanthan gum
- 1 tsp baking powder
- 1 /2 tsp dough enhancer
- 1 /8 tsp ascorbic acid
- 2 ½ tsp. salt

WET INGREDIENTS

- 2/3 cup of milk warmed to about 80°F
- 1 ½ stick unsalted butter, melted and slightly cooled
- 4 large eggs, whisked
- 2 tsp apple cider vinegar

Step-by-Step Directions to Cook It:

1. Add milk, egg, butter, and vinegar to a bowl and mix
2. Add the yeast to a bowl and set aside
3. Add flour, xanthan gum, milk powder, baking powder, dough enhancer, sugar, and ascorbic acid in a pan
4. Pour the liquid ingredients in the Cuisinart bread pan, spread the Dry ingredients over it
5. Make a shallow well in the center and add the yeast
6. insert Cuisinart bread pan back to the Cuisinart Bread Machine
7. Close the lid and Select program: white.
8. Select Crust color: medium and Loaf size 1 ½-lb; press the start button
9. Remove bread and allow to cool; serve, and enjoy.

Serving Suggestion: use to prepare French toast
Preparation and Cooking Tips: make sure the butter and milk are not too hot
Nutritional value per serving: Calories: 210kcal, Fat: 10g, Carb: 25g, Proteins: 5g

Traditional Egg Bread

Traditional egg bread is rich and tasty bread. The egg adds a certain lushness to the outcome of this recipe

Prep time: 5 minutes

Cooking time: 3 hours 25 minutes

Serves: 1 Loaf

Ingredients To Use:

DRY INGREDIENTS

- 2 ¼ cups of bread flour
- 1 ¼ cup of millet flour
- 2 tbsp. active dry yeast
- 1 /4 cup of milk powder
- 2 tbsp. sugar
- 2 ½ tsp baking powder
- 1 tsp xanthan gum
- 1 /8 tsp ascorbic acid
- 1 /2 tsp salt

WET INGREDIENTS

- 3 large eggs, whisked
- 6 tbsp. salted butter, melted and slightly cooled
- 1 tbsp. honey
- ¾ cup of water, warmed
- 2 tsp apple cider vinegar

Step-by-Step Directions to Cook It:

1. Mix honey and water, add the remaining wet ingredients and mix
2. Measure the yeast and set it aside. Add all the dry ingredients and mix
3. Pour the liquid ingredients into the Cuisinart bread pan; spread the Dry ingredients on it
4. Make a shallow well in the center and add the yeast
5. insert Cuisinart bread pan back to the Cuisinart Bread Machine
6. Close the lid and Select program; White.
7. Select Crust color; medium and Loaf size; 1 ½-lb. press the start button
8. Remove bread and allow to cool; serve, and enjoy.

Serving Suggestion: serve with strawberry jam

Preparation and Cooking Tips: Makes sure the eggs are at room temperature

Nutritional value per serving: Calories: 241kcal, Fat: 15g, Carb: 29g, Proteins: 17g

Almost Wheat Sandwich Bread

This bread is closely related to the wheat bread in terms of flavor. Sorghum and flax seeds add extra flavor, and it is rich in fiber

Prep time: 5 minutes
Cooking time: 3hours 25 minutes
Serves: 1 Loaf

Ingredients To Use:

DRY INGREDIENTS

- 2 cups of bread flour
- 2 tbsp. active dry yeast
- 1 cup of sorghum flour
- 1 /2 cup of milk powder
- 3 tbsp. sugar
- ¼ cup of flaxseed meal
- 1 ½ tsp salt
- 2 tsp baking powder
- 2 tsp xanthan gum

WET INGREDIENTS

- 1 cup of plus 2 tbsp. warm water
- 3 large eggs, whisked
- 2 tsp apple cider vinegar
- 3 tbsp. olive oil

Step-by-Step Directions to Cook It:

1. Add water, egg, vinegar, olive oil, and whisk together
2. Add yeast to a bowl and set aside. Add bread flour, sorghum flour, milk powder, baking powder, salt, and flaxseed meal in a bowl. Mix until well combined
3. Pour the liquid ingredients into the Cuisinart bread pan; spread the Dry ingredients over it
4. Make a shallow well in the center and add the yeast
5. insert Cuisinart bread pan back to the Cuisinart Bread Machine
6. Close the lid and Select program; White
7. Select Crust color; medium and Loaf size; 1 ½-lb. press the start button
8. Remove bread and allow to cool; serve, and enjoy.

Serving Suggestion: serve with mixed berry jam

Preparation and Cooking Tips: you may add ascorbic acid

Nutritional valuc pcr serving: Calories: 241kcal, Fat: 12g, Carb: 34g, Proteins: 16g

Potato Bread

This potato bread is denser and flavorful. The potato adds nutrients and flavor to the bread. It also helps keep it moist for a longer time

Prep time: 5 minutes

Cooking time: 3hours 25minutes

Serves: 1 Loaf

Ingredients To Use:

DRY INGREDIENTS

- 2 ½ cup of whole-grain flour
- 1 tbsp instant yeast
- 2 tsp tapioca flour
- ½ cup of potato starch
- 1 /2 cup of milk powder
- 2 tbsp. sugar
- 2 tsp psyllium husk flakes
- 2 tsp salt

WET INGREDIENTS

- ½ cup of mashed potatoes
- 2 large eggs, whisked
- ¼ cup of warm water
- 2 tsp apple cider vinegar
- 2 tbsp butter, melted and slightly cooled.

Step-by-Step Directions to Cook It:

1. add egg, water, vinegar, butter, and whisk. Add the potatoes and mix until smooth
2. Measure the yeast and set it aside. Mix all the dry ingredients in a bowl
3. Pour the liquid ingredients into the Cuisinart bread pan; spread the Dry ingredients over it
4. Make a shallow well in the center and add the yeast
5. insert Cuisinart bread pan back to the Cuisinart Bread Machine
6. Close the lid and Select program; White.
7. Select Crust color; Medium, and Loaf size;1 ½-lb. press the start button
8. Remove bread and allow to cool; serve, and enjoy.

Serving Suggestion: Serve with chicken salad

Preparation and Cooking Tips: use Yukon gold potatoes for a golden loaf

Nutritional value per serving: Calories: 211kcal, Fat: 16g, Carb: 34g, Proteins: 10g

Sorghum Oat-Buttermilk Bread

The bread is a combination of rich and distinct flavors. It is tender, soft, and highly nutritious; the buttermilk gives it a cream color. The oats add to the texture.

Prep time: 5 minutes

Cooking time: 3 hours 25 minutes

Serves: 1 Loaf

Ingredients To Use:

DRY INGREDIENTS

- 1 ½ cup of sorghum flour
- 1 cup of bread flour
- ½ cup of oat flour
- 3 tbsp. sugar
- ½ cup of buttermilk powder
- 2 tsp xanthan gum
- 4 tsp active dry yeast
- 1 ½ tsp baking powder
- 1 /2 tsp baking soda
- 1 /8 tsp ascorbic acid
- 2 tsp salt

WET INGREDIENTS

- 2 tsp honey
- 3 large eggs, whisked
- 1 tbsp. apple cider Vinegar
- 1 cup of plus 2 tbsp. warm water
- ¼ cup of olive oil

Step-by-Step Directions to Cook It:

1. Mix water and honey in a bowl, add egg, olive, vinegar, and whisk
2. Add dry ingredients to a pan and mix
3. Pour the liquid ingredients in the Cuisinart bread pan, spread the Dry ingredients over it
4. Make a shallow well in the center and add the yeast
5. insert Cuisinart bread pan back to the Cuisinart Bread Machine
6. Close the lid and Select program: white.
7. Select Crust color: medium and Loaf size;1 ½-lb. press the start button
8. Remove bread and allow to cool; serve, and enjoy.

Serving Suggestion: Serve alongside scrambled egg

Preparation and Cooking Tips: If the dough is too wet, add a small amount of flour

Nutritional value per serving: Calories: 321kcal, Fat: 13g, Carb: 28.6g, Proteins: 14g

Golden Millet Bread

Golden Miller bread is a tender flavored bread with an attractive golden color. It is rich and can be enjoyed in quite a number of ways.

Prep time: 5 minutes
Cooking time: 3 hours 25 minutes
Serves: 1 Loaf

Ingredients To Use:

Dry ingredients

- 1 cup of bread flour
- 1 ½ cup of millet flour
- ½ cup of sorghum flour
- 4 tsp active dry yeast
- ½ cup of buttermilk powder
- ¼ cup of sugar
- 2 tsp xanthan gum
- 1 ½ tsp baking powder
- 1 /8 tsp ascorbic acid
- 2 tsp salt

Wet ingredients

- 3 large eggs, whisked
- 1 tsp apple cider vinegar
- ¼ cup of olive oil
- 1 cup of warm water

Step-by-Step Directions to Cook It:

1. add egg, vinegar, oil, and water in a pan; whisk until smooth
2. Add the yeast to a bowl and set aside. Add all the dry ingredients to a bowl and mix
3. Pour the liquid ingredients into the Cuisinart bread pan, then the Dry ingredients
4. Make a shallow well in the center and add the yeast
5. insert Cuisinart bread pan back to the Cuisinart Bread Machine
6. Close the lid and Select program; white.
7. Select Crust color: Medium and Loaf size;1 ½-lb. press the start button
8. Remove bread and allow to cool; serve, and enjoy.

Serving Suggestion: serve toasted with peanut butter

Preparation and Cooking Tips: eggs must be at room temperature

Nutritional value per serving: Calories: 241kcal, Fat: 12g, Carb: 26g, Proteins: 13g

CHAPTER 3: VEGETABLE BREAD

Scallion and Cilantro Cornbread

This savory cornbread has a lot going for it in the flavor department. It is rich and nutritious, with scallion and cilantro adding flavor to it.

Prep time: 5 minutes
Cooking time: 4 hours 5 minutes
Serves: 1 Loaf

Ingredients To Use:

DRY INGREDIENTS

- 2 cups of bread flour
- 1 cup of cornflour
- ¼ cup of. sugar
- 1 tbsp baking powder
- 1 tsp kosher salt
- 1 tsp xanthan gum
- 2 scallions, finely chopped
- 1 tbsp chopped fresh cilantro

WET INGREDIENTS

- 3 large eggs, whisked
- ¼ cup of. Veg oil
- 1 cup of warm water

Step-by-Step Directions to Cook It:

1. Add eggs, veg oil, and warm water in a bowl; mix
2. Add bread flour, cornflour, sugar, salt, baking powder, and xanthan gum in a bowl and mix
3. Pour the liquid ingredients into the Cuisinart bread pan, spread the flour mixture over it
4. Add the yeast and insert the Cuisinart bread pan back to the Cuisinart Bread Machine
5. Close the lid and Select program; Ultra-fast.
6. Select Crust color; medium, and Loaf size; 1 ½-lb press the start button
7. After the Kneading process, press the start button. Open the lid and remove the Cuisinart bread pan
8. Remove the kneading paddle; add the cilantro and scallion. Reshape the dough
9. Press the start button to resume the program. Remove and allow to cool; serve

Serving Suggestion: serve with grilled bratwurst.
Preparation and Cooking Tips: ingredients must be at room temperature
Nutritional value per serving: Calories: 187kcal, Fat: 10g, Carb: 23g, Proteins: 16g

Caramelized Onion Bread

Caramelized onion bread is quite popular in Frace and is used to prepare snacks or dishes. The onions add a subtle flavor and sweetness to the bread

Prep time: 5 minutes

Cooking time: 4 hours 5minutes

Serves: 1 Loaf

Ingredients To Use:

DRY INGREDIENTS

- 3 cups of bread flour
- 2 tbsp. active dry yeast
- ½ cup of. Milk powder
- 1 tbsp baking powder
- 2 tbsp. sugar
- 2 tsp xanthan gum
- 1/8 tsp ascorbic acid
- 1 tsp kosher salt

WET INGREDIENTS

- 1 cup of caramelized onion
- 3 large eggs, whisked
- 1 cup of. Warm water
- 2 tsp ume plum vinegar
- ¼ cup of vegetable oil

Step-by-Step Directions to Cook It:

1. Mix water, egg, vinegar, and oil in a bowl. Stir in the onions
2. Add yeast to a bowl and set aside. Mix all the dry ingredients in another bowl
3. Pour the liquid ingredients in the Cuisinart bread pan, spread the Dry ingredients over it
4. Make a shallow well in the center and add the yeast
5. insert Cuisinart bread pan back to the Cuisinart Bread Machine
6. Close the lid and Select program; whole wheat.
7. Select Crust color; medium and Loaf size;1 ½-lb. press the start button
8. Remove bread and allow to cool; serve, and enjoy.

Serving Suggestion: Stuff with salad and serve

Preparation and Cooking Tips: All ingredients must be at room temperature

Nutritional value per serving: Calories: 214kcal, Fat: 9g, Carb: 23g, Proteins: 11g

Roasted Garlic Bread

The aroma of the roasted garlic bread is simply enticing, and the sweetness is perfect. The right amount to enjoy your salad

Prep time: 5 minutes

Cooking time: 4 hours 5minutes

Serves: 1 Loaf

Ingredients To Use:

DRY INGREDIENTS

- 2 cups of whole wheat flour
- 1 /2 cup of milk powder
- 2 tsp xanthan gum
- 2 tbsp. active dry yeast
- 2 tbsp. sugar
- 1 tbsp baking powder
- 1 /8 tsp ascorbic acid
- 1 tsp kosher salt

WET INGREDIENTS

- 2 Cloves of Roasted Garlic, peeled and minced
- 1 cup of plus 3 tbsp. warm water
- ¼ cup of. olive oil
- 2 large eggs, whisked
- 2 tsp apple cider vinegar

Step-by-Step Directions to Cook It:

1. Mix water with egg, oil, and vinegar. Stir in the garlic.
2. Add the yeast to a bowl and set aside. Mix all the dry ingredients in another bowl
3. Pour the liquid ingredients in the Cuisinart bread pan, spread the Dry ingredients over it
4. Make a shallow well in the center and add the yeast
5. insert Cuisinart bread pan back to the Cuisinart Bread Machine
6. Close the lid and Select program: Whole Wheat.
7. Select Crust color: medium, and Loaf size;1 ½-lb press the start button
8. Remove bread and allow to cool; serve, and enjoy.

Serving Suggestion: Serve with salami

Preparation and Cooking Tips: the ingredients must be evenly distributed.

Nutritional value per serving: Calories: 178kcal, Fat: 9g, Carb: 27g, Proteins: 9g

Olive and Oregano Bread

Everyone loves the Mediterranean flavor, and their aromas are tantalizing.

Prep time: 5 minutes
Cooking time: 4 hours 5 minutes
Serves: 1 Loaf

Ingredients To Use:

DRY INGREDIENTS

- 2 cups of bread flour
- 2 tbsp. active dry yeast
- 1 cup of. millet flour
- ¼ cup of. sugar
- 1 tbsp baking powder
- 2 tsp psyllium powder
- 1 tsp dried oregano
- 1 /8 tsp ascorbic acid
- 1 tsp kosher salt

Wet Ingredients

- 1 cup of Niçoise olives, pitted
- 1 cup of plus 3 tbsp. warm water
- 2 large eggs, whisked
- 2 tsp apple cider vinegar
- ¼ cup of vegetable oil

Step-by-Step Directions to Cook It:

1. add water, vinegar, egg, oil to a pan and combine. Stir in the olives,
2. add the yeast in a bowl, and set aside. Add bread flour, millet flour, sugar, salt, baking powder, ascorbic acid, oregano, and psyllium powder in a pan and mix.
3. Pour the liquid ingredients in the Cuisinart bread pan, spread the Dry ingredients over it
4. Make a shallow well in the center and add the yeast
5. insert Cuisinart bread pan back to the Cuisinart Bread Machine
6. Close the lid and Select program: white.
7. Select Crust color: medium, and Loaf size;1 ½-lb. press the start button
8. Remove bread and allow to cool; serve, and enjoy.

Serving Suggestion: serve with bouillabaisse

Preparation and Cooking Tips: olive must be pitted

Nutritional value per serving: Calories: 231kcal, Fat: 11g, Carb: 32g, Proteins: 19g

Tomato Bread

Tomato bread is delicious with a saucy taste that takes your tongue on a ride. You can get creative and shape it into a baguette.

Prep time: 5 minutes

Cooking time: 4 hours 5 minutes

Serves: 1 Loaf 1 loaf

Ingredients To Use:

Dry ingredients

- 2 ¾ cups of bread flour
- ½ cup of whole wheat flour
- 1 ½ tbsps gluten
- 2 tsp active dry yeast
- 1 ½ tsp salt

Wet ingredients

- 1/3 cup of chopped oil-packed, sun-dried tomatoes
- 1 ¼ cups of water
- 3 tbsps tomato paste

Step-by-Step Directions to Cook It:

1. add water, tomato paste, chopped tomatoes in a pan and mix
2. Add wheat flour, bread flour, gluten, salt in a pan and mix
3. Pour the tomato mixture into the Cuisinart bread pan, then add the flour mixture
4. Make a shallow well in the center and add the yeast
5. insert Cuisinart bread pan back to the Cuisinart Bread Machine
6. Close the lid and Select program: Whole Wheat.
7. Select Crust color: Medium and Loaf size;1 ½-lb. press the start button
8. Remove bread and allow to cool; serve, and enjoy.

Serving Suggestion: serve with grilled cheese

Preparation and Cooking Tips: use dry tomatoes

Nutritional value per serving: Calories: 321kcal, Fat: 21g, Carb: 36g, Proteins: 21g

Zucchini bread

The zucchini bread contributes to a healthy dinner meal; besides, the Zucchini adds moisture and flavor to the dough.

Prep time: 5 minutes

Cooking time: 4 hours 5 minutes

Serves: 1 Loaf

Ingredients To Use:

Dry ingredients

- 2 cups of bread flour
- 1 cup of whole wheat flour
- 1 tbsp. gluten
- 2 tsp yeast
- 1 ½ tsp salt
- 1 tbsp. dark brown sugar

Wet ingredients

- 1 cup of shredded Zucchini
- 3/4 cup of fat-free milk
- Zest of 1 lemon (grated)
- 2 tbsp. olive oil

Step-by-Step Directions to Cook It:

1. add olive oil, milk, lemon zest, and mix. Add the Zucchini, and combine
2. Add bread flour, wheat flour, gluten, salt, sugar, and mix.
3. Pour the milk mixture into the Cuisinart bread pan, then the Dry ingredients
4. Make a shallow well in the center and add the yeast
5. insert Cuisinart bread pan back to the Cuisinart Bread Machine
6. Close the lid and Select program: Whole wheat.
7. Select Crust color: Medium and Loaf size;1 ½-lb press the start button
8. Remove bread and allow to cool; serve, and enjoy.

Serving Suggestion: Serve with grilled cheese

Preparation and Cooking Tips: use shredded Zucchini

Nutritional value per serving: Calories: 123kcal, Fat: 10g, Carb: 23g, Proteins: 15g

Pumpkin Bread

It's winter season; get ready to enjoy the goodness of the pumpkin bread. Pumpkin has a distinct flavor, and it has moisture in the dough.

Prep time: 5 minutes

Cooking time:4 hours 5minutes

Serves: 1 Loaf

Ingredients To Use:

Dry ingredients

- 4 ½ cups of all-purpose flour
- 3 tbsp granulated sugar
- 2 tsp salt
- 2 tsp. Active dry yeast

Wet ingredients

- Grated zest of 1 orange
- 1 cup of canned pumpkin puree
- ½ cup of water
- 1/3 cup of butter, melted
- ½ cup of milk

Step-by-Step Directions to Cook It:

1. add the orange zest, water, butter, milk, pumpkin puree, and mix
2. Add flour, sugar, salt, and mix
3. Pour the pumpkin mixture into the Cuisinart bread pan, then spread the flour mixture
4. Make a shallow well in the center and add the yeast
5. insert Cuisinart bread pan back to the Cuisinart Bread Machine
6. Close the lid and Select program: Whole wheat.
7. Select Crust color; medium, and Loaf size;1 ½-lb. press the start button
8. Remove bread and allow to cool; serve, and enjoy.

Serving Suggestion: serve with scrambled egg

Preparation and Cooking Tips: You can also use winter squash.

Nutritional value per serving: Calories: 271kcal, Fat: 12g, Carb: 34g, Proteins: 14g

Lemon-Leek Loaf

The combination of lemon and leek is sure to make a flavorful bread. They both have distinct tastes and aromas, which are infused into the bread.

Prep time: 5 minutes

Cooking time: 4 hours 5 minutes

Serves: 1 Loaf

Ingredients To Use:

Dry ingredients

- ½ tsp baking soda
- 2 cups of unbleached flour, all-purpose
- ½ tsp salt
- ½ tsp baking powder
- ½ tsp of freshly ground black pepper

Wet ingredients

- 1 tbsp of butter, unsalted
- 2 cups of chopped leeks, cooked in butter
- 4 large eggs, whisked
- 1½ cups of sour cream
- 1 tbsp grated lemon zest

Step-by-Step Directions to Cook It:

1. Add flour, baking powder, baking soda, and salt in a bowl, mix
2. Add butter, leeks, egg, sour cream, and lemon zest; mix.
3. Pour the leek mixture into the Cuisinart bread pan; then the flour mixture
4. insert Cuisinart bread pan back to the Cuisinart Bread Machine
5. Close the lid and Select program.
6. Select Crust color: medium and Loaf size;1 ½-lb. press the start button
7. Remove bread and allow to cool; serve, and enjoy.

Serving Suggestion: Serve with fish

Preparation and Cooking Tips: cook leek until soft

Nutritional value per serving: Calories: 197kcal, Fat: 13g, Carb: 24g, Proteins: 12g

CHAPTER 4: FRUIT BREAD

Zucchini-Applesauce Bread

This bread recipe is a blend of vegetables and fruit with a dash of spice. You can say this bread as it all, and it tastes great too.

Prep time: 5 minutes

Cooking time: 4 hours 5minutes

Serves: 1 Loaf

Ingredients To Use:

Dry ingredients

- 1 ½ cup of bread flour
- 1 cup of millet flour
- 2 tsp baking powder
- 1 ¼ cup of granulated sugar
- 2 tsp psyllium husk flakes
- 3 /4 tsp ground cinnamon
- 1 tsp salt
- ½ cup of chocolate chips

Wet ingredients

- 1 cup of grated peeled Zucchini
- 3 large eggs, whisked
- 1/3 cup of vegetable oil
- 2 tsp pure vanilla extract
- ½ cup of applesauce

Step-by-Step Directions to Cook It:

1. Whisk oil, egg, vanilla, applesauce, and Zucchini in a bowl
2. Add all the dry ingredients except yeast and chocolate chips to a bowl
3. Pour the zucchini mixture into the Cuisinart bread pan, then the dry ingredients
4. insert Cuisinart bread pan back to the Cuisinart Bread Machine
5. Close the lid and Select program: ultra-fast.
6. Select Crust color; medium and Loaf size;1 ½-lb. press the start button
7. Press pause after the knead cycle; add the chocolate chips. Select start to continue the program
8. Remove bread and allow to cool; serve, and enjoy.

Serving Suggestion: serve with scrambled egg

Preparation and Cooking Tips: egg must be at room temperature

Nutritional value per serving: Calories: 234kcal, Fat: 12g, Carb: 21g, Proteins: 13g

Raspberry Quick Bread

Raspberry is known for its sweet and delicious taste. When incorporated in the bread gives it a rich taste and color.

Prep time: 5 minutes

Cooking time: 2 hours 3minutes

Serves: 1 Loaf

Ingredients To Use:

Dry ingredients

- 2 cups of bread flour
- 1 cup of millet flour
- 1 cup of granulated sugar
- 1 tbsp baking powder
- 1 tbsp psyllium husk flakes or powder
- 1 tsp kosher or fine sea salt

Wet ingredients

- ½ cup of warm unsweetened coconut milk
- 1 /4 cup of vegetable oil
- 2 tsp pure vanilla extract
- 2 large eggs, whisked
- 1 1/3 fresh raspberry

Step-by-Step Directions to Cook It:

1. Mix coconut milk, vanilla, oil, and eggs in a bowl
2. Mix bread flour, millet flour, sugar, baking powder, and psyllium husk in a bowl.
3. Pour the wet ingredients into the Cuisinart bread pan, then the Dry ingredients
4. insert Cuisinart bread pan back to the Cuisinart Bread Machine
5. Close the lid and Select program; ultra-fast.
6. Select Crust color: light and Loaf size;1 ½-lb. press the start button
7. After the first knead cycle, add the raspberry, continue the program
8. Remove bread and allow to cool; serve, and enjoy.

Serving Suggestion: Serve as a sandwich

Preparation and Cooking Tips: the egg should be at room temperature before use

Nutritional value per serving: Calories: 267kcal, Fat: 10g, Carb: 21g, Proteins: 11g

Pineapple-Coconut Bread

This bread contains two unlikely flavors, but surprisingly it turns out great. Rich in flavor and aroma with a sweet taste that you are going to enjoy.

Prep time: 5 minutes
Cooking time: 2hours 5minutues
Serves: 1 Loaf

Ingredients To Use:

Dry ingredients

- 2 ½ cup of bread flour
- ½ cup of coconut flour
- 1 cup of granulated sugar
- 2 tsp baking powder
- 1 tbsp psyllium powder
- 1 tsp salt

Wet ingredients

- 2 cups of sweetened shredded coconut
- 1 cup of warmed unsweetened coconut milk
- 3 large eggs, whisked
- 1/3 cup of vegetable oil
- 2 tsp pure vanilla extract
- 1 cup of chopped pineapple

Step-by-Step Directions to Cook It:

1. Mix all the wet ingredients in a pan except shredded coconut and chopped pineapple
2. Mix all the dry ingredients in a bowl except the yeast
3. Pour the wet ingredients into the Cuisinart bread pan, then the Dry ingredients
4. insert Cuisinart bread pan back to the Cuisinart Bread Machine
5. Close the lid and Select program: ultra-fast.
6. Select Crust color; medium, and Loaf size;1 ½-lb press the start button
7. Press pause after the first knead cycle, add the pineapple and coconut. Resume the program.
8. Remove bread and allow to cool; serve, and enjoy.

Serving Suggestion: serve as toast

Preparation and Cooking Tips: add water if the dough is too wet

Nutritional value per serving: Calories: 236kcal, Fat: 10g, Carb: 24g, Proteins: 9g

Cherry-Wheat Berry Bread

Get creative with this wonderful bread with a sweet and delicious taste. Enjoy the flavor of cherry and wheat berry for Thanksgiving.

Prep time: 5 minutes
Cooking time: 2 hours 5 minutes
Serves: 1 Loaf

Ingredients To Use:

Dry ingredients

- 3 cups of bread flour
- 2 ½ tsp. Active dry yeast
- 2 tsp gluten
- 1 ½ tsp salt

Wet ingredients

- 1 cup of water
- 1/4 cup of honey
- 1 large egg white, whisked
- 2 tbsp canola oil
- 1/2 cup of tart dried cherries tossed with 1 tbsp. flour
- 1/3 cup of wheat berries

Step-by-Step Directions to Cook It:

1. Mix water, honey, egg, oil in a bowl
2. Mix flour, gluten, salt in another bowl
3. Pour the wet ingredients into the Cuisinart bread pan, then the Dry ingredients
4. Make a shallow well in the center and add the yeast
5. insert Cuisinart bread pan back to the Cuisinart Bread Machine
6. Close the lid and Select program; ultra-fast.
7. Select Crust color; medium, and Loaf size;1 ½-lb. press the start button
8. After the first knead cycle, add the tart cherries and wheat berries. Resume the program.
9. Remove bread and allow to cool; serve, and enjoy.

Serving Suggestion: Serve as a chicken sandwich

Preparation and Cooking Tips: recipe not suitable for the delayed timer

Nutritional value per serving: Calories: 193kcal, Fat: 10g, Carb: 23g, Proteins: 9g

Apricot walnut sweet Bread

Apricot walnut sweet bread is a delicious bread that is perfect for breakfast. It can also be used in the preparation of other snacks.

Prep time: 5 minutes

Cooking time: 2 hours 5 minutes

Serves: 1 Loaf

Ingredients To Use:

Dry ingredients

- 2 ¼ cup of bread flour
- 1 cup of granulated sugar
- 1 tsp ground ginger
- ¾ cup of millet flour
- 2 tsp psyllium powder
- 1 tbsp baking powder
- 1 /2 tsp salt

Wet ingredients

- ½ cup of toasted walnut, chopped
- 1 /4 cup of vegetable oil
- ½ cup of warm water or apricot nectar
- 1 cup of chopped dried apricots
- 3 large eggs, whisked

Step-by-Step Directions to Cook It:

1. Mix flour, sugar, ginger, millet flour, psyllium powder, baking powder, and salt in a bowl.
2. Mix oil, water, apricots, egg, and walnut in a bowl
3. Pour the wet ingredients into the Cuisinart bread pan, then the Dry ingredients
4. insert Cuisinart bread pan back to the Cuisinart Bread Machine
5. Close the lid and Select program: white.
6. Select Crust color: Light and Loaf size;1 ½-lb. press the start button
7. Remove bread and allow to cool; serve, and enjoy.

Serving Suggestion: serve with tea

Preparation and Cooking Tips: steep the apricot in hot boiling water

Nutritional value per serving: Calories: 256kcal, Fat: 14g, Carb: 22g, Proteins: 8g

Blueberry Quick Bread

The blueberry in this recipe is the perfect blend with the brown sugar; it balances the sweetness with its tangy taste.

Prep time: 5 minutes

Cooking time: 2 hours 5 minutes

Serves: 1 Loaf

Ingredients To Use:

Dry ingredients

- 1 ½ cup of bread flour
- 1 cup of millet flour
- 1 cup of granulated sugar
- 1 tbsp baking powder
- 2 tsp psyllium powder
- 1 tsp salt

Wet ingredients

- ½ cup of warm unsweetened coconut milk
- 1 tsp pure vanilla extract
- 1/3 cup of vegetable oil
- 3 large eggs, whisked
- 1 ¼ cup of fresh blueberries, rinsed and patted dry

Step-by-Step Directions to Cook It:

1. Mix coconut milk, vanilla extract, oil, eggs in a bowl
2. Mix flour, baking powder, sugar, psyllium powder, and salt in a bowl
3. Pour the wet ingredients into the Cuisinart bread pan, then the Dry ingredients
4. insert Cuisinart bread pan back to the Cuisinart Bread Machine
5. Close the lid and Select program; ultra-fast.
6. Select Crust color: medium and Loaf size;1 ½-lb. press the start button
7. Press pause after the first knead cycle, add the blueberries and resume the program.
8. Remove bread and allow to cool; serve, and enjoy.

Serving Suggestion: Serve with any topping of choice

Preparation and Cooking Tips: when using dry blueberries, steep with hot water

Nutritional value per serving: Calories: 258kcal, Fat: 10g, Carb: 21g, Proteins: 11g

Cranberry-orange Bread

Cranberry sauce is always an all-time favorite; now you can create that flavor in loaves of bread using this recipe. The orange adds a mild flavor to the bread too.

Prep time: 5 minutes

Cooking time: 4hours 5minutes

Serves: 1 Loaf

Ingredients To Use:

Dry ingredients

- 3 cups of bread flour
- 1 tbsp psyllium powder
- 2 tbsp. active dry yeast
- 2 tsp baking powder
- ¾ cup of granulated sugar
- 1 tsp salt
- 1 /8 tsp ascorbic acid

Wet ingredients

- 3 large eggs, whisked
- 2 tsp apple cider vinegar
- ½ cup of orange juice
- ½ cup of warm water
- ¼ cup of vegetable
- 2 cup of fresh cranberries

Step-by-Step Directions to Cook It:

1. Mix bread flour, psyllium powder, sugar, salt, ascorbic acid, and baking powder in a bowl
2. Mix eggs, vinegar, juice, oil in a bowl. Add the cranberries and mix
3. Pour the wet ingredients into the Cuisinart bread pan, then the Dry ingredients
4. Make a shallow well in the center and add the yeast
5. insert Cuisinart bread pan back to the Cuisinart Bread Machine
6. Close the lid and Select program; whole wheat.
7. Select Crust color; medium, and Loaf size;1 ½-lb. press the start button
8. Remove bread and allow to cool; serve, and enjoy.

Serving Suggestion: prepare as a turkey sandwich

Preparation and Cooking Tips: all ingredients must be at room temperature

Nutritional value per serving: Calories: 246kcal, Fat: 10g, Carb: 26g, Proteins: 8g

Lemon Quick Bread

There is nothing like a delightful lemony aroma, and this bread gives the full lemon flavor. Enjoy as a light dessert.

Prep time: 5 minutes

Cooking time: 4hours 5 minutes

Serves: 1 Loaf

Ingredients To Use:

Dry ingredients

- 2 ½ cup of bread flour
- ½ cup of almond flour
- ¼ cup of sugar
- 1 /2 cup of coconut milk powder
- 1 tbsp psyllium powder
- 11 tbsp baking powder
- 1 tsp salt

Wet ingredients

- ½ cup of freshly squeezed lemon juice
- 3 large eggs, whisked
- Grated zest of 1 lemon
- 1/3 cup of vegetable oil

Step-by-Step Directions to Cook It:

1. Mix lemon juice, lemon zest, egg, and oil in a bowl.
2. Mix almond flour, bread flour, milk powder, baking powder, psyllium powder, sugar, and salt in a bowl.
3. Pour the wet ingredients in the Cuisinart bread pan; then the Dry ingredients
4. insert Cuisinart bread pan back to the Cuisinart Bread Machine
5. Close the lid and Select program: whole wheat.
6. Select Crust color; medium. and Loaf size;1 ½-lb. press the start button
7. Remove bread and allow to cool; serve, and enjoy.

Serving Suggestion: serve with lemon glaze

Preparation and Cooking Tips: all ingredients must be at room temperature

Nutritional value per serving: Calories: 253kcal, Fat: 8g, Carb: 27g, Proteins: 13g

CHAPTER 5: CHEESE BREAD

Cottage Cheese and Dill Bread

Have you ever had a bread that is so cheesy and spicy? Here is one for the cheese lovers. You are going to love this bread

Prep time: 5 minutes

Cooking time: 3hours 25 minutes

Serves: 1 Loaf

Ingredients To Use:

Dry ingredients

- 2 ½ cups of bread flour
- 1 tbsp sugar
- 2 tbsp dried dill weed
- 1 tbsp gluten
- 2 tsp. Yeast
- 1 ¼ tsp salt

Wet ingredients

- 2 tbsp olive oil
- 1/4 cup of fat-free milk
- 1 medium shallot, chopped and cooked
- 1 cup of cottage cheese
- 1 large egg

Step-by-Step Directions to Cook It:

1. Mix oil, milk, shallot, cheese, and egg in a bowl
2. Mix flour, sugar, dill weed, gluten, and salt in a bowl.
3. Pour the liquid ingredients into the Cuisinart bread pan, then the Dry ingredients
4. Make a shallow well in the center and add the yeast
5. insert Cuisinart bread pan back to the Cuisinart Bread Machine
6. Close the lid and Select program: White.
7. Select Crust color; dark and Loaf size;1 ½-lb. press the start button
8. Remove bread and allow to cool; serve, and enjoy.

Serving Suggestion: Serve with bread pudding

Preparation and Cooking Tips: sauté the shallot

Nutritional value per serving: Calories: 217kcal, Fat: 9g, Carb: 21g, Proteins: 17g

Buttermilk Cheese Bread

Swiss cheese is known for there hole-like texture but with a unique flavor associated with it. The breast has an enticing flavor that goes well with Jam.

Prep time: 5 minutes

Cooking time: 3 hours 25minutes

Serves: 1 Loaf

Ingredients To Use:

Dry ingredients

- 3 ½ cups of bread flour
- 1 ½ tbsp sugar
- 1 ½ tsp salt
- 2 tsp active dry yeast
- 1 ¼ tsp baking powder

Wet ingredients

- 1 cup of shredded Swiss cheese
- 1 cup of buttermilk
- 1/2 cup of water

Step-by-Step Directions to Cook It:

1. Mix flour, sugar, salt, and baking powder in a bowl.
2. Mix buttermilk, swiss cheese, and water in another bowl
3. Pour the wet ingredients into the Cuisinart bread pan, then the Dry ingredients
4. Make a shallow well in the center and add the yeast
5. insert Cuisinart bread pan back to the Cuisinart Bread Machine
6. Close the lid and Select program: white.
7. Select Crust color; medium and Loaf size;1 ½-lb. press the start button
8. Remove bread and allow to cool; serve, and enjoy.

Serving Suggestion: serve with meat soup

Preparation and Cooking Tips: the recipe must not be used with a delayed timer

Nutritional value per serving: Calories: 246kcal, Fat: 10g, Carb: 24g, Proteins: 16g

Asiago Cheese Bread

Asiago cheese bread is common everywhere, with its attractive, sharp, and distinct small. Everywhere smells nice when preparing this bread.

Prep time: 5 minutes

Cooking time: 3 hours 25 minutes

Serves: 1 Loaf

Ingredients To Use:

Dry ingredients

- 3 ¼ cups of bread flour
- 2 tsp yeast
- 1 ½ tbsp milk powder
- 1 tbsp sugar
- 2 tsp gluten
- 1/2 tsp salt

Wet ingredients

- 3/4 cup of grated Asiago cheese
- 3 large eggs
- 1/2 cup of plus 1 tbsp water
- 3 tbsp olive oil

Step-by-Step Directions to Cook It:

1. Mix bread flour, sugar, milk, gluten, and salt.
2. Mix asiago cheese, eggs, water, and olive oil
3. Pour the wet ingredients into the Cuisinart bread pan, then the Dry ingredients
4. Make a shallow well in the center and add the yeast
5. insert Cuisinart bread pan back to the Cuisinart Bread Machine
6. Close the lid and Select program.
7. Select Crust color; medium. and Loaf size;1 ½-lb. press the start button
8. Remove bread and allow to cool; serve, and enjoy.

Serving Suggestion: serve with chili soup

Preparation and Cooking Tips: all ingredients must be at room temperature

Nutritional value per serving: Calories: 254kcal, Fat: 10g, Carb: 25g, Proteins: 9g

Parmesan Nut Bread

Parmesan is an all-time favorite, and incorporating the nice flavor into a loaf of bread is the ultimate. Better enjoyed as Sandwich.

Prep time: 5 minutes

Cooking time: 3 hours 25 minutes

Serves: 1 Loaf

Ingredients To Use:

Dry ingredients

- 3 cups of bread flour
- 1/2 tsp salt
- 1 tbsp gluten
- Pinch of sugar
- 2 tsp active dry yeast

Wet ingredients

- 1 cup of water
- 1 ½ tbsp olive oil
- 2/3 cup of grated Parmesan cheese
- 1/3 cup of pine nuts, coarsely chopped
- 1/2 cup of walnuts, coarsely chopped

Step-by-Step Directions to Cook It:

1. Mix flour, salt, gluten, sugar in a bowl.
2. Mix water, oil, and parmesan in a bowl
3. Pour the wet ingredients into the Cuisinart bread pan, then the Dry ingredients
4. Make a shallow well in the center and add the yeast
5. insert Cuisinart bread pan back to the Cuisinart Bread Machine
6. Close the lid and Select program; white.
7. Select Crust color; medium and Loaf size; 1 ½-lb. press the start button
8. After the kneading cycle, add the pine nuts and the walnuts. Resume the program
9. Remove bread and allow to cool; serve, and enjoy.

Serving Suggestion: serve with salad

Preparation and Cooking Tips: all ingredients must be at the room temperature

Nutritional value per serving: Calories: kcal, Fat: g, Carb: g, Proteins: g

Blue Cheese and Walnut Bread

The blue cheese and walnut bread is a beautiful and pleasant piece of bread that tastes delicious. The cheese adds flavor and texture to the bread.

Prep time: 5 minutes

Cooking time: 3 hours 25 minutes

Serves: 1 Loaf

Ingredients To Use:

Dry ingredients

- 2 cups of bread flour
- 1 cup of wheat flour
- 2 tbsp active dry yeast
- ½ cup of milk powder
- 3 tbsp granulated sugar
- 1 tbsp baking powder
- 1 /8 tsp ascorbic acid
- 2 tsp xanthan gum
- 1 tsp salt

Wet ingredients

- 3 large eggs, whisked
- 1 cup of warm water
- 2 tsp apple cider vinegar
- 3 tbsp vegetable oil
- ¾ cup of crumbled blue cheese
- 1 cup of chopped toasted walnuts

Step-by-Step Directions to Cook It:

1. Mix all the dry ingredients except the yeast.
2. Mix egg, water, vinegar, oil, and blue cheese in a bowl.
3. Pour the wet ingredients into the Cuisinart bread pan, then the Dry ingredients
4. Make a shallow well in the center and add the yeast
5. insert Cuisinart bread pan back to the Cuisinart Bread Machine
6. Close the lid and Select program: white.
7. Select Crust color; medium, and Loaf size; 1 ½-lb. press the start button
8. Pause after the knead cycle, add the toasted walnut.
9. Remove bread and allow to cool; serve, and enjoy.

Serving Suggestion: serve with tomato-based soup

Preparation and Cooking Tips: all ingredients must be at room temperature

Nutritional value per serving: Calories: 257kcal, Fat: 17g, Carb: 28g, Proteins: 15g

Ricotta and Fresh Chives Bread

This is one bread to make for your first attempt, simple and easy. The fresh chives add a subtle flavor to the bread.

Prep time: 5 minutes
Cooking time: 3hours 25 minutes
Serves: 1 Loaf

Ingredients To Use:

Dry ingredients

- 3 cups of bread flour
- 1 tbsp light brown sugar
- 1 tbsp gluten
- 1/2 cup of chopped fresh chives
- 2 ½ tsp active dry yeast
- Dash of ground black pepper
- 1 ½ tsp salt

Wet ingredients

- 1 cup of water
- 1/3 cup of whole ricotta cheese

Step-by-Step Directions to Cook It:

1. Mix water and cheese in a pan
2. Mix bread flour, brown sugar, gluten, fresh chives, black pepper, and salt
3. Pour the liquid ingredients into the Cuisinart bread pan, then the Dry ingredients
4. Make a shallow well in the center and add the yeast
5. insert Cuisinart bread pan back to the Cuisinart Bread Machine
6. Close the lid and Select program; white.
7. Select Crust color; medium, and Loaf size;1 ½-lb. press the start button
8. Remove bread and allow to cool; serve, and enjoy.

Serving Suggestion: serve with pasta dishes

Preparation and Cooking Tips: grate the cheese

Nutritional value per serving: Calories: kcal, Fat: g, Carb: g, Proteins: g

Cottage Cheese Bread

Cottage cheese is common in rural areas where fresh milk is readily available. Enjoy the fresh flavor of the bread.

Prep time: 5 minutes
Cooking time: 3 hours 25 minutes
Serves: 1 Loaf

Ingredients To Use:

Dry ingredients

- 2 ½ cups of bread flour
- 1/2 cup of whole wheat flour
- 1 tsp. active dry yeast
- 2 tbsp sugar
- 1 tbsp gluten
- 1 ½ tsp salt

Wet ingredients

- 3/4 cup of cottage cheese
- 3/4 cup of water
- 2 tbsp. olive oil

Step-by-Step Directions to Cook It:

1. Mix oil, cheese, and water in a pan
2. Mix all the dry ingredients except the yeast.
3. Pour the wet ingredients into the Cuisinart bread pan, then the Dry ingredients
4. Make a shallow well in the center and add the yeast
5. insert Cuisinart bread pan back to the Cuisinart Bread Machine
6. Close the lid and Select program; white.
7. Select Crust color; medium, and Loaf size;1 ½-lb. press the start button
8. Remove bread and allow to cool; serve, and enjoy.

Serving Suggestion: serve with Jam
Preparation and Cooking Tips: all ingredients must be at room temperature
Nutritional value per serving: Calories: 187kcal, Fat: 10g, Carb: 20g, Proteins: 7g

Roquefort Cheese Bread

This is another cheese bread that you are going to enjoy immensely. It infuses the bread with its strong salty taste.

Prep time: 5 minutes

Cooking time: 3 hours, 25 minutes

Serves: 1 Loaf

Ingredients To Use:

Dry ingredients

- 2 ¾ cups of bread flour
- 1/4 cup of medium or dark rye flour
- 1 tbsp gluten
- 1 tbsp light brown sugar
- 1/2 tsp salt
- 2 tsp active dry yeast

Wet ingredients

- 1 cup of water
- 2 tbsp cream sherry
- 1/2 cup of chopped pecans
- ¼ cup of Roquefort cheese, crumbled
- 1 tbsp walnut oil
- 1 tbsp unsalted butter, cut into pieces

Step-by-Step Directions to Cook It:

1. Add all the wet ingredients to a pan
2. Add all the dry ingredients in a pan except yeast.
3. Pour the wet ingredients into the Cuisinart bread pan, then the Dry ingredients
4. Make a shallow well in the center and add the yeast
5. insert Cuisinart bread pan back to the Cuisinart Bread Machine
6. Close the lid and Select program; white.
7. Select Crust color; medium, and Loaf size;1 ½-lb. press the start button
8. Remove bread and allow to cool; serve, and enjoy.

Serving Suggestion: serve with pear and red wine

Preparation and Cooking Tips: all ingredients must be at room temperature

Nutritional value per serving: Calories: 187kcal, Fat: 10g, Carb: 19g, Proteins: 7g

CHAPTER 6: HERB AND SPICE BREAD

Cuisinart Rye Bread

Rye bread is tasty. It is crusty on the outside and soft inside. It can be enjoyed with grilled cheese, sandwiches, and many more.

Preparation time: 30 minutes
Cooking time: 40 minutes
Serves: 2 loaves

Ingredients To Use:

Dry Ingredients

- 1 tsp of active dry yeast
- Rye flour
- Bread flour
- ¼ cup of unsweetened cocoa powder
- 1 tbsp of caraway seed
- 2 tbsp of brown sugar
- 1 tbsp of baking powder
- 1 tbsp of salt

Liquid ingredients

- 2½ cups of tepid water
- ¼ cups of vegetable oil
- 2/3 cup of unsulphured molasses
- 3 large eggs.

Step-by-Step Directions to Cook It:

1. Set the paddle into the bread pan and insert it into the Cuisinart Bread Machine
2. Pour warm water into a bowl, and add molasses. Whisk until molasses dissolves.
3. Pour tepid water, vegetable oil, dissolved molasses, and eggs into the bread pan, after which you add the bread flour, rye flour, baking powder, salt, caraway seed, and unsweetened cocoa powder.
4. Make a hole in the center of the mixture and add the yeast.
5. Select medium crust and select the knead cycle and leave to rise.
6. Choose the baking program and set the timer for 1 hour.
7. At the end of the bake cycle, check if the temperature is 99 ∘ c. At that temperature, the bread is ready.
8. Remove the pan from the Cuisinart Bread Machine and place it on a cooling rack.

Serving suggestions: serve with grilled cheese.
Preparation and Cooking Tips: caraway seeds are optional.
Nutritional value per serving: Calories:259 kcal, Fat:3.3 g, Carb:48 g, Prot:9g

Cheddar Cheese and Chives bread

Cheddar cheese and chives bread is a masterpiece. It is cheesy, puffy with a soft inner and crispy exterior.

Preparation time: 20 minutes
Cooking time: 35 minutes
Serves: 5

Ingredients To Use:

- 2½ tsp of active dry yeast
- 4 cups of bread flour
- ½ cups of granulated sugar
- 1 baking soda
- 8 Tbsp of unsalted butter.
- Shredded cheddar cheese

Liquid ingredients

- 2 big eggs
- 2 cup of tepid water

Step-by-Step Directions to Cook It:

1. Set the paddle at the bottom of the bread pan.
2. Add 2 cups of tepid water and whisked eggs to the bread pan, after which, you add the unsalted butter, sugar, baking soda, shredded cheddar cheese, and bread flour.
3. Make a hole in the center and add the yeast.
4. Insert the bread pan into the Cuisinart Bread Machine
5. Close the lid
6. Select the dough program to knead and rise the dough.
7. Bring out the dough and remove the paddle from the bottom of the bread pan.
8. Mold the dough into a round form, return to the pan, and select the bake program
9. Select medium crust and 1½ lb loaf size; press the start button and wait until the bread is done.
10. Allow bread to cool.

Serving suggestions: Serve with casseroles

Preparation and Cooking Tips: bread flour is best for making cheddars.

Cinnamon Raisin Bread

Cinnamon raisin bread is a delicious loaf filled with raisins. It is perfect for making toasts

Preparation time: 15 minutes

Cooking time: 3 hours

Serves: 4

Ingredients To Use:

Liquid ingredients

- ¾ liquid cup of lukewarm milk
- 1/3 cup of tepid water
- 28g of melted butter

Dry ingredients

- ½ cup of raisins or any dry fruit of your choice
- ½ cup of rolled oats
- 1 of baking soda
- 2½ tsp of instant yeasts
- 3 cups of all-purpose flour
- 1¼ cup of brown sugar
- ¼ tsp of salt

Step-by-Step Directions to Cook It:

1. Set the paddle at the bottom of the bread pan
2. To the bread pan, add warm water of lukewarm milk, melted butter, after which, you add the salt, baking soda, raisin fruit, rolled oats, brown sugar, and all-purpose flour.
3. Make a hole in the center and add the yeast.
4. Insert the bread pan into the Cuisinart Bread Machine
5. Close the lid
6. Select the dough program to knead and rise the dough.
7. Bring out the dough and remove the paddle from the bottom of the bread pan.
8. Mold the dough into a round form, put it back into the pan, and select the bake program.
9. Select dark crust and 1½ lb loaf size; press the start button and wait until the bread is done.

Serving suggestions: Top with cinnamons

Preparation and Cooking Tips: toast with softened butter

Onion and Cumin Bread

This recipe results in a tasty and delightful bread with cumin and onion fillings.

Preparation time: 35minutes

Cooking time: 2 hours

Serves: 5

Ingredients To Use:

Dry ingredient

- 250g of bread flour
- 10g of yeast
- 10g of salt
- Chopped onions
- 1 tsp of baking

Liquid Ingredients

- 2 Tbsp of oil
- 2 cups of lukewarm water

Step-by-Step Directions to Cook It:

1. To the bread pan, add 2 cups of lukewarm water, olive oil after which, you add the salt, baking soda, chopped onions, and bread flour
2. Make a hole in the center and add the yeast.
3. Insert the bread pan into the Cuisinart Bread Machine
4. Close the lid
5. Select the dough program to knead and rise the dough.
6. Bring out the dough and remove the paddle from the bottom of the bread pan.
7. Mold the dough into a round form, return to the pan, and select the bake program
8. Select dark crust and 1½ lb loaf size; press the start button and wait until the bread is done.

Serving suggestions: serve with salad or soup

Preparation and Cooking Tips: all-purpose flour can be used in place of bread flour.

Italian Herb Bread

Italian herb bread is fluffy, delicious, and can be served as dinner.

Preparation time: 30 minutes

Cooking time: 35 minutes

Serves: 5

Ingredients To Use:

Dry ingredients

- 10g of yeast
- 1 tbsp of salt
- 1 tsp of baking soda
- 1 tsp of garlic powder
- 6 cups of bread flour
- 1 tbsp of dried oregano
- White sugar
- 1 tsp of dried basil

Liquid ingredients

- Diced Romanic cheese
- 2 cups of warm water
- ¼ cup of olive oil

Step-by-Step Directions to Cook It:

1. To the bread pan, add 2 cups of warm water, olive oil.
2. Add the sugar, salt, cheese, garlic powder, baking soda, oregano, dried basil, and flour.
3. Make a hole in the center and add the yeast.
4. Insert the bread pan into the Cuisinart Bread Machine
5. Close the lid
6. Select the dough program to knead and rise the dough
7. Bring out the dough and remove the paddle from the bottom of the bread pan.
8. Mold the dough into a round form, return to the pan, and select the bake program
9. Select color medium and 1½ lb loaf size; press the start button and allow the bread to cook. Remove the bread and allow cooling.

Serving suggestions: Drizzle with olive oil

Preparation and Cooking Tips: All-purpose flour can be used instead of bread flour.

Rosemary Bread

Rosemary bread is a delicious bread. It has a crispy feel in the mouth and can be eaten at any time of the day.

Preparation time: 15 minutes

Cooking time: 1 hour 15 minutes

Serves: 3

Ingredients To Use:

Dry ingredients

- 2½ cups of flour
- 1 tsp baking soda
- 1 tsp of salt
- 1 tsp of sugar
- 1 tsp of rosemary

Wet ingredients

- 1 cup of tepid water
- 2 tsp of melted butter

Step-by-Step Directions to Cook It:

1. Add 1 cup of tepid water, 2 tsp of melted butter, sugar, salt, baking soda, rosemary, and all-purpose flour to the bread pan.
2. Make a hole in the center and add the yeast.
3. Insert the bread pan into the Cuisinart Bread Machine
4. Close the lid
5. Select the dough program to knead and rise the dough
6. Bring out the dough and remove the paddle from the bottom of the bread pan.
7. Mold the dough into a round form, put it back into the pan, and select the bake program.
8. Select color light and 1 lb loaf size; press the start button and wait until the bread is done.
9. Allow bread to cool.

Serving suggestions: Serve with salad

Preparation and Cooking Tips: bread flour can also be used in place of all-purpose flour.

Orange and Cloves Bread

This recipe results in a loaf of delicious orange bread. It is cake-like and excellent for gatherings and other special occasions.

Preparation time: 15 minutes

Cooking time: 50 minutes

Serves: 2

Ingredients To Use:

Dry ingredients

- 2¼ cups of bread flour
- yeast
- 1 tsp of baking soda
- 1 tsp of orange zest
- 1 tsp of whole cloves

Wet ingredients

- 1 cup of chopped oranges
- 1 cup of melted butter
- 1 cup of maple syrup
- 3 eggs
- 1 cup of warm water

Step-by-Step Directions to Cook It:

1. To the bread pan, add a cup of warm water, chopped oranges, melted butter, maple syrup, eggs, after which, you add the salt, baking soda, orange zest, cloves, and bread flour.
2. Make a hole in the center and add the yeast.
3. Insert the bread pan into the Cuisinart Bread Machine
4. Close the lid
5. Select the dough program to knead and rise the dough.
6. Bring out the dough and remove the paddle from the bottom of the bread pan.
7. Mold the dough into a round form, return to the pan, and select the bake program.
8. Select dark crust and 1½ lb loaf size; press the start button and wait until the bread is done.
9. Place bread on a wire rack and allow cooling.

Serving suggestions: Serve with almonds

Preparation and Cooking Tips: ripe oranges are best for this recipe.

Cuisinart Cumin Bread

Cumin bread is tasty and can be enjoyed with butter spread as dinner or breakfast.

Preparation time: 25 minutes

Cooking time: 45 minutes

Serves: 4

Ingredients To Use:

Dry ingredients

- 1½ cups of all-purpose flour
- 2 tbsp of sugar
- 1 tbsp of baking powder
- 2 tsp of ground cumin
- ¼ tsp of dry mustard
- 1 tsp of salt

Wet ingredients

- 2/3 cup of fat free-milk
- 2 tbsp of vegetable oil
- 1 cup of warm water.

Step-by-Step Directions to Cook It:

1. Set paddle at the bottom of the bread pan of Cuisinart Bread Machine
2. To the bread pan, add milk, warm water, vegetable oil, after which, you add the salt, dry mustard, sugar, ground cumin, and all-purpose flour.
3. Make a hole in the center and add the yeast.
4. Insert the bread pan into the Cuisinart Bread Machine
5. Close the lid
6. Select the dough program to knead and rise the dough.
7. Bring out the dough and remove the paddle from the bottom of the bread pan.
8. Mold the dough into a round form, return to the pan, and select the bake program.
9. Select medium crust and 1½ lb loaf size; press the start button and wait until the bread is done.
10. Remove bread from the bread pan and wait until it's cool.

Serving suggestions: enjoy with jam or butter spread

Preparation and Cooking Tips: bread flour can be used

CHAPTER 7: SWEET BREAD

Cuisinart Banana bread

Banana bread is sweet, moist, and tastes like cake. It can be enjoyed as breakfast or lunch.

Preparation time: 15 minutes
Cooking time: 2 hours 10 minutes
Serves: 4

Ingredients To Use:

Dry ingredients

- 1 tsp of sugar
- 1 tsp of baking powder
- 1 tsp of brown sugar
- 1 cup of flour
- 1 tsp of salt

Wet ingredients

- 4 eggs
- 1 cup of tepid water
- 1 cup of mashed bananas
- 1 cup of olive oil
- 1 cup of milk

Step-by-Step Directions to Cook It:

1. Set paddle at the bottom of the bread pan
2. Pour into the bread pan the tepid water, milk, eggs, oil, mashed bananas.
3. Also, add the flour, brown and white sugar, baking powder, salt, and flour into the bread pan.
4. Fix the bread pan into the Cuisinart Bread Machine
5. Select the quick bread program and set the timer for 2 hours.
6. After 2hours, select the baking only program and set the timer for 10minutes
7. Remove the bread from the machine and allow it to cool.

Serving suggestions: Enjoy with jam or butter spread.

Preparation and Cooking Tips: Ripe bananas are the best for this recipe

Cuisinart Cardamom Bread

Cardamom bread is usually served during traditional holidays in Sweden. It is delicious and has a pleasant aroma

Preparation time: 1 hour 30 minutes

Cooking time: 30 minutes

Serves: 2

Ingredients To Use:

- 2 cups of whole milk
- ½ cup of unsalted butter
- 2 packets of active dry yeast
- 2/3 cup of granulated sugar
- 6 cups of all-purpose flour
- 1 tsp of kosher salt
- 2 tsp of ground cardamom
- 2 large eggs
- 2 tbsp of pearl sugar

Step-by-Step Directions to Cook It:

1. In a bowl, add milk, egg, sugar and whisk until sugar dissolves. Add melted butter and whisk all together.
2. Ensure the milk mixture is warm, then add the yeast to the milk mixture.
3. Wait for minutes and confirm if yeast is active.
4. Pour mixture into the bread pan and fix into the Cuisinart Bread Machine
5. Add salt, cardamom, and flour.
6. Close the lid and select the kneading program.
7. Always check if the dough is sticky. If the dough is sticky, add some flour.
8. After the kneading cycle, leave the dough to rise.
9. After the dough is doubled in size, remove it from the machine and place it on a flat surface.
10. Cut dough into three parts and form three tiny ropes
11. Bring all three ropes close and braid them.

10\. To the bread pan, add a cup of warm water, chopped oranges, melted butter, maple syrup, eggs, after which, you add the salt, baking soda, orange zest, cloves, and bread flour.

11\. Make a hole in the center and add the yeast.

12. Insert the bread pan into the Cuisinart Bread Machine
13. Close the lid
14. Select the dough program to knead and rise the dough.
15. Bring out the dough and remove the paddle from the bottom of the bread pan. Mold the dough into a round form, return to the pan, and select the bake program.
16. Select dark crust and 1½ lb loaf size; press the start button and wait until the bread is done. Place bread on a wire rack and allow cooling.
12. When the bread is done, allow cooling.

Serving suggestions: Enjoy with coffee

Preparation and Cooking Tips: Mold the dough and bake.

Hungarian Sweet Bread

Hungarian sweet bread is elegant and delicious. It is a traditional bread eaten as part of a daily meal

Preparation time: 90minutes

Cooking time: 40minutes

Serves: 7

Ingredients To Use:

- 400 ml of warm milk
- 12 tsp of sugar
- 25 of fresh yeast.
- 650g of all-purpose flour
- 1 egg
- ¼ tsp of salt

Step-by-Step Directions to Cook It:

1. In a bowl, add milk, egg, sugar and whisk until sugar dissolves. Add melted butter and whisk all together.
2. Ensure the milk mixture is warm, pour in your yeast in the milk mixture.
3. Wait for minutes and confirm if yeast is active.
4. Pour mixture into the bread pan and fix into the Cuisinart Bread Machine
5. Add salt, cardamom, and flour.
6. Close the lid and select the kneading program.
7. Always check if the dough is sticky. If the dough is sticky, add some flour.
8. After the kneading cycle, leave the dough to rise.
9. After the dough is doubled in size, remove it from the machine and place it on a flat surface.
10. Mold into balls
11. Use egg white to brush the dough's surface, return it to the Cuisinart Bread Machine, select the baking option, and set the timer for an hour.
12. When the bread is done, allow cooling.

Serving suggestions: Enjoy with tea or coffee.

Preparation and Cooking Tips: ensure yield proofs before you go ahead to bake.

Cuisinart Manchet

Manchet is a classic bread. It is delicious and healthy.

Preparation time: 25 minutes

Cooking time: 50 minutes

Serves: 3

Ingredients To Use:

- 2 ounce of white flour
- 2 tsp of salt
- 20g of yeast
- Warm milk
- 1 egg
- Baking powder

Step-by-Step Directions to Cook It:

1. Add a cup of warm milk and eggs to the bread pan,
2. Add the salt, baking soda, and bread flour.
3. Make a hole in the center and add the yeast.
4. Insert the bread pan into the Cuisinart Bread Machine
5. Close the lid
6. Select the dough program to knead and rise the dough.
7. Bring out the dough and remove the paddle from the bottom of the bread pan.
8. Mold the dough into a round form and brush with egg white. Put back into the pan, and select the bake program.
9. Select dark crust and 1½ lb loaf size; press the start button and wait until the bread is done.
10. Place bread on a wire rack and allow cooling
11. Mold the dough into a round form, return to the pan, and select the bake program.
12. Select dark crust and 1½ lb loaf size; press the start button and wait until the bread is done.

12. Place bread on a wire rack and allow cooling.

Serving suggestions: Enjoy plain.

Preparation and Cooking Tips: bread flour can also be used

Pineapple Bun

Pineapple buns are classic. They are soft, sweet, and crispy.
Preparation time: 35 minutes
Cooking time: 1hour
Serves: 4

Ingredients To Use:

- 2/3 cup of cream
- 1 big egg
- 3 tsp of sugar
- 1 tbsp of active yeast.
- 1 tsp of salt
- 1 cup of milk
- 1 tsp of baking soda
- ½ tsp of vanilla extract
- 2 cups of bread flour
- 1 tsp of pineapple flavor.

Step-by-Step Directions to Cook It:

1. Set paddle at the bottom of the bread pan
2. Pour into the bread pan the milk, eggs, cream, and pineapple flavor.
3. Also, add the flour, sugar, baking powder, and salt into the bread pan.
4. Fix the bread pan into the Cuisinart Bread Machine
5. Select the quick bread program and set the timer for 2hours.
6. After 2hours, select the baking only program and set the timer for 10 minutes
7. Bring out bread from the machine and allow it to cool

Serving suggestions: Enjoy with fruit juice.
Preparation and Cooking Tips: all-purpose flour can also be used to bake.

Raisin Bread

Raisin bread is filled with raisins and often flavored with cinnamon. It is delicious and an excellent choice for breakfast.

Preparation time: 20 minutes

Cooking time: 25minutes

Serves: 8

Ingredients To Use:

- ¼ ounce of active yeast
- ¼ cup of tepid water
- ¼ cup of softened butter
- ¼ cup of granulated sugar
- 1 cup of milk
- 2 cups of all-purpose flour
- 1 tsp baking soda
- 1 cup of raisins
- ½ tsp of salt
- 2 eggs

Step-by-Step Directions to Cook It:

1. To the bread pan, add a cup of tepid water, milk, and softened butter, after which, you add the sugar, salt, baking soda, raisins, and all-purpose flour.
2. Make a hole in the center and add the yeast.
3. Insert the bread pan into the Cuisinart Bread Machine
4. Close the lid.
5. Select the dough program to knead and rise the dough.
6. Bring out the dough and remove the paddle from the bottom of the bread pan.
7. Mold the dough into a round form, return to the pan, and select the bake program.
8. Select color light and 1 lb loaf size; press the start button and wait until the bread is done.
9. Allow bread to cool.

Serving suggestions: Serve at any time of the day

Preparation and Cooking Tips: flavor with cinnamon

Cuisinart Strawberry Bread

Strawberry bread is a beautiful and delicious dessert-easy to make
Preparation time: 10 minutes
Cooking time: 2 hours
Serves: 6

Ingredients To Use:

- ¼ cup of softened butter
- 1 egg
- 2 tsp of baking powder
- 2 cups of all-purpose flour
- ½ tsp of salt
- ½ tsp of vanilla
- 1½ cups of chopped strawberry
- ½ cup of milk.

Step-by-Step Directions to Cook It:

1. Set paddle at the bottom of the bread pan
2. Pour into the bread pan the vanilla, milk, eggs, butter, chopped strawberries.
3. Also, add the sugar, yeast and salt, baking powder, and flour into the bread pan.
4. Fix the bread pan into the Cuisinart Bread Machine
5. Select the quick bread program and set the timer for 1hour.
6. After 1 hour, select the baking only program and set the timer for 12 minutes
7. Bring out bread from the machine and allow it to cool.

Serving suggestions: can be glazed with icing sugar
Preparation and Cooking Tips: Ensure ripe strawberries are used.

Cuisinart Cozonac

Cozonac is a simple sweetened bread with origins in Romania.

Preparation time: 20 minutes

Cooking time: 60 minutes

Serves: 4

Ingredients To Use:

- 1 cup of milk
- 6 cups of bread flour
- ¾ cup of granulated sugar
- ½ cup of softened butter
- 2 tbsp of dry yeast
- 1 tbsp of orange and lemon zest each.
- ½ tsp of salt
- 1 tbsp of baking powder

Step-by-Step Directions to Cook It:

1. Set paddle at the bottom of the bread pan of Cuisinart Bread Machine
2. To the bread pan, add milk, warm water, and butter.
3. Add the salt, baking powder, sugar, orange and lemon zest, and bread flour.
4. Make a hole in the center and add the yeast.
5. Insert the bread pan into the Cuisinart Bread Machine
6. Close the lid
7. Select the dough program to knead and rise the dough.
8. Bring out the dough and remove the paddle from the bottom of the bread pan.
9. Mold the dough into a round form, return to the pan, and select the bake program
10. Select dark crust and 1lb loaf size; press the start button and wait until the bread is done.

Serving suggestions: slightly whisked eggs can be used as toppings

Preparation and Cooking Tips: all-purpose flour can bake the bread in the absence of bread flour.

CHAPTER 8: SOURDOUGH BREAD

Cuisinart Sourdough Bread

Sourdough bread is a hard crust bread; it has a tangy and sour taste.

Preparation time: 8 hours 25 minutes

Cooking time: 5 hours

Serves: 5

Ingredients To Use:

- ¾ tbsp of sourdough starter
- 3 cups of bread flour
- ½ tbsp of sugar
- 1¾ tsp of salt.
- 1 cup of tepid water

Step-by-Step Directions to Cook It:

1. Set paddle into the bottom of the bread pan.
2. Add tepid water, flour, sugar, sourdough starter.
3. Insert bread pan into the Cuisinart Bread Machine and close the lid.
4. Press the start button and select the dough program to knead and rise the dough
5. Set the timer for 3hours.
6. Leave the dough in the Cuisinart Bread Machine for 8 hours.
7. Bring out dough and Mold into a round loaf with your hands and put back into the bread making machine
8. Select the bake program for the medium crust at 1 lb size.
9. Set the timer for 5 hours.
10. When the bread is done, allow cooling.

Serving suggestions: strong white flour can be used in place of bread flour.

Preparation and Cooking Tips: can be eaten with shallots

Rustic Sourdough Bread

Rustic sourdough bread is a chewy loaf with rich flavor and mild tang.

Preparation time: 12 minutes

Cooking time: 30 minutes

Serves: 9

Ingredients To Use:

- 1 cup of tepid water
- 2 tsp of salt
- 1 tsp of instant yeast
- 5 cups of all-purpose flour
- 227g of sourdough starter

Step-by-Step Directions to Cook It:

1. Set the paddle at the bottom of the bread pan.
2. Add the tepid water, sourdough starter, flour, salt, and yeast.
3. Insert bread pan into the Cuisinart Bread Machine and close the lid and press the start button.
4. Select the dough program to knead and rise the dough
5. Set the timer for 2hours
6. After the knead and rise cycle is over, select the bake program and set the timer for 5 hours.
7. When the bread is done, bring it out to cool.

Serving suggestions: Enjoy with butter spread.

Preparation and Cooking Tips: bread flour can also be used.

Sourdough Focaccia

Sourdough focaccia is an Italian loaf with a chewy and tangy taste.
Preparation time: 35 minutes
Cooking time: 3hours
Serves: 4

Ingredients To Use

- 1 tsp of kosher salt
- 2 tsp of active dry yeast
- 150g of flour blend
- 1 tbsp of sugar
- 0.8oz of milk powder
- 2 tsp of psyllium powder
- 180ml of sourdough starter
- 2 eggs
- 60ml of warm water
- 1 tbsp of vegetable oil
- 2 tsp of apple cider vinegar

Step-by-Step Directions to Cook It:

1. Set the paddle at the bottom of the bread pan and add warm water, oil, vinegar, sourdough starter, eggs.
2. Add flour, milk, psyllium, salt, and yeast.
3. Insert bread pan into the Cuisinart Bread Machine and close lid.
4. Select the kneading cycle. Allow to knead for 2o minutes and allow 2 rise cycles for 40 minutes.
5. After the kneading and rise cycle is over, select the bake program and select medium or dark crust.
6. Select bread size to 1 1½ lb loaf and set the timer for 1hour.
7. When the bread is done, bring it out to cool.

Serving suggestions: Enjoy plain or with olive oil.
Preparation and Cooking Tips: Ensure sourdough starter is bubbly

Potato Sourdough Bread

Potato sourdough bread has a tangy and sweet taste. It is rich in flavor.

Preparation time: 15 minutes
Cooking time: 1 hour
Serves: 8

Ingredients To Use:

- 1 cup of sourdough starter
- 4 cups of lukewarm water
- 7 cups of bread flour
- 2 tsp of salt
- 1 cup of plain mashed potatoes
- 1/3 cup of oil
- 1/3 cup of sugar

Step-by-Step Directions to Cook It:

1. Set the paddle at the bottom of the bread pan and add lukewarm water, oil, mashed potatoes, sourdough starter.
2. Add flour, salt, and yeast.
3. Insert bread pan into the Cuisinart Bread Machine and close lid.
4. Select the kneading cycle. Allow to knead for 2o minutes and allow 2 rise cycles for 40 minutes.
5. After the kneading and rise cycle is over, select the bake program and select medium or dark crust.
6. Select bread size to 1½ lb loaf and set the timer for 1hour.
7. When the bread is done, bring it out to cool.

Serving suggestions: Enjoy plain

Preparation and Cooking Tips: melted butter or margarine can be used instead of oil.

Danish Rye Sourdough Bread

Danish rye sourdough bread is delicious. It is perfect for sandwiches.

Preparation time: 30 minutes

Cooking time: 1hour 15 minutes

Serves: 3

Ingredients To Use:

- Sourdough starter
- 250g dark rye flour
- 130g bread flour
- 2 cups of warm water
- 1 tbsp of salt
- 2 tbsp of molasses

Step-by-Step Directions to Cook It:

1. Set the paddle at the bottom of the bread pan and pour in warm water and sourdough starter.
2. Add flour, rye flour, salt, molasses, and yeast.
3. Insert bread pan into the Cuisinart Bread Machine and close lid.
4. Select the kneading cycle. Allow to knead and rise. Set the timer for 15minutes
5. After the kneading and rise cycle is over, select the bake program and select medium or dark crust. Set the timer for 1hour.
6. Select bread size to 1½ lb loaf and set the timer for 1hour.
7. When the bread is done, bring it out to cool.

Serving suggestions: use as bread for the sandwich

Preparation and Cooking Tips: strong white flour or all-purpose flour can also be used.

Honey Wheat and Sourdough Bread

Honey wheat and sourdough bread is made from whole wheat grains. It can be enjoyed at any time of the day.

Preparation time: 25minutes

Cooking time: 1hour

Serves: 8

Ingredients To Use:

- 1 cup of active sourdough starter
- 2 cup of bread flour
- 1 cup of warm water
- 2 tbsp of honey
- 1 tbsp of salt
- 7.5oz of ground whole wheat flour
- 1 egg
- Sesame seeds

Step-by-Step Directions to Cook It:

1. Set the paddle at the bottom of the bread pan and add warm water, honey, sourdough starter, eggs.
2. Add flour, wheat flour, and salt.
3. Insert bread pan into the Cuisinart Bread Machine and close lid.
4. Select the kneading cycle. Allow kneading for 20 minutes.
5. After the kneading and rise cycle is over, bring out dough and brush with egg, and put it back into the machine.
6. Select the bake program and select dark crust.
7. Select bread size to 1 lb loaf and set the timer for 1hour.
8. When the bread is done, bring it out to cool.

Serving suggestions: can be eaten with honey

Preparation and Cooking Tips: sesame seeds are optional

Sourdough Pumpernickel Bread

Sourdough pumpernickel bread is a whole new level of deliciousness.

Preparation time: 25 minutes

Cooking time: 60minutes

Serves: 5

Ingredients To Use:

- 21g of dry yeast
- 165g of flour
- 95g of buckwheat
- 2 tbsp of brown sugar
- 2 tsp of unsweetened cocoa powder
- 2tsp of baking powder
- Sourdough starter
- 1 tbsp of olive oil
- 3 eggs
- 1 cup of warm water.

Step-by-Step Directions to Cook It:

1. Set paddle into the bottom of the bread pan.
2. Add tepid water, oil, sourdough starter, baking powder, wheat flour, cocoa powder, flour, sugar, and yeasts.
3. Insert bread pan into the Cuisinart Bread Machine and close the lid.
4. Select the dough program to knead and rise the dough. Set the timer for 2hours.
5. Leave the dough in the Cuisinart Bread Machine for 8hours.
6. Bring out dough and Mold into a round loaf with your hands and put back into the bread making machine
7. Select the bake program and select dark crust and 1 lb size. After which, you set the timer for 1hours.
8. When the bread is done, bring it out to cool.

Serving suggestions: Enjoy with soup

Preparation and Cooking Tips: bread or all-purpose flour can also be used **for** baking

Sourdough Ciabatta

Sourdough ciabatta is a delightful Italian bread.
Preparation time: 15 minutes
Cooking time: 2 hours
Serves: 5

Ingredients To Use:

- 4 tsp of dry yeast
- 355g of whole grain flour or light flour
- 35g of granulated sugar
- 2 tsp of salt
- 2 tsp of psyllium powder
- 1 cup of sourdough starter
- 90ml of warm water
- 45ml of vegetable oil

Step-by-Step Directions to Cook It:

1. Set paddle into the bottom of the bread pan.
2. Add tepid water and vegetable oil.
3. Add salt, flour, sugar, sourdough starter, psyllium powder, whole grain flour, and yeast.
4. Insert bread pan into the Cuisinart Bread Machine and close the lid.
5. Select the dough program to knead and rise the dough
6. Set the timer for 1 hour.
7. Leave the dough in the Cuisinart Bread Machine for 3hours.
8. Bring out dough and Mold into a round loaf with your hands and put back into the bread making machine
9. Select the bake program and select medium crust and 1 lb size. After which, you set the timer for 45minutes.
10. When the bread is done, bring it out to cool.

Serving suggestions: coarse sea salt can be used as toppings

Preparation and Cooking Tips: light flour or whole grain flour can be used for baking

CHAPTER 9: RED MEAT BREAD

Chorizo and Cheddar Bread

This is our favorite taco turned bread; it is so cheesy and delicious, and you won't be able to resist a second serving.

Prep time: 5 minutes

Cooking time: 4 hours 5 minutes

Serves: 1 Loaf

Ingredients To Use:

Dry ingredients

- 2 tbsp.active dry yeast
- 2 cups of bread flour
- 1 ½ cup of. cornflour
- 2 tbsp. Granulated sugar
- 1 tbsp baking powder
- 1 tsp kosher salt
- 1 tsp xanthan gum

Wet ingredients

- 1 /4 cup of vegetable oil
- 3 large eggs, whisked
- ¾ cup of water
- 2 tsp apple cider vinegar
- ¾ cup of shredded cheddar cheese
- 6 oz. chorizo, crumbled and cooked

Step-by-Step Directions to Cook It:

1. Mix all the wet ingredients in a pan
2. Mix all the dry ingredients in a pan except the yeast
3. Pour the liquid ingredients into the Cuisinart bread pan, then the Dry ingredients
4. Make a shallow well in the center and add the yeast
5. insert Cuisinart bread pan back to the Cuisinart Bread Machine
6. Close the lid and Select program; Whole Wheat.
7. Select Crust color: medium and Loaf size;1 ½-lb press the start button
8. Remove bread and allow to cool; serve, and enjoy.

Serving Suggestion: Serve with hot chili sauce

Preparation and Cooking Tips: cook the chorizo on medium heat and drain

Bacon Cheese Savoury Bread

The bread is moist, crispy, and soft, perfect for celebrating thanksgiving dinner. Enjoy with any side dish of choice

Prep time: 5 minutes

Cooking time: 3 hours 25 minutes

Serves: 1 Loaf

Ingredients To Use:

Dry ingredients

- 1 ¼ cup of wheat flour
- 2 tsp baking powder
- 2 tsp. Active dry yeast.
- 1/2 tsp baking soda
- 1 cup of bread flour
- 1 tsp of salt

Wet ingredients

- 7 crispy bacon strips chopped
- 2 eggs
- 2 1/2 tbsp. olive oil
- ¼ cup of shredded cheddar cheese
- 1 ¼ cups of buttermilk

Step-by-Step Directions to Cook It:

1. Mix eggs, oil, cheese, buttermilk in a pan, add the bacon, and mix.
2. Mix wheat flour, baking powder, bread flour, and salt in a bowl
3. Pour the wet ingredients into the Cuisinart bread pan, then the Dry ingredients
4. Make a shallow well in the center and add the yeas
5. insert Cuisinart bread pan back to the Cuisinart Bread Machine
6. Close the lid and Select program: white.
7. Select Crust color: medium and Loaf size;1 1/2-lb press the start button
8. Remove bread and allow to cool; serve, and enjoy.

Serving Suggestion: serve with salad

Preparation and Cooking Tips: all ingredients must be at room temperature.

Chorizo Bread

The chorizo bread is a classic Mediterranean bread that can serve as a good appetizer. It is tender and fluffy.

Prep time: 5 minutes

Cooking time: 3hours 25 minutes

Serves: 1 Loaf

Ingredients To Use:

Dry ingredients

- 1 ¼ cup of wheat flour
- 2 tsp baking powder
- 2 tsp. Active dry yeast.
- 1 cup of chorizo sausage, chopped
- 1 cup of bread flour
- 1 tsp of salt

Wet ingredients

- 2 1/2 tbsp. olive oil
- ¼ cup of shredded cheddar cheese
- 1 ¼ cups of warm water

Step-by-Step Directions to Cook It:

1. Mix oil, cheese, and warm water in a pan
2. Mix wheat flour, chorizo, baking powder, bread flour, and salt in a bowl
3. Pour the wet ingredients into the Cuisinart bread pan, then the Dry ingredients
4. Make a shallow well in the center and add the yeas
5. insert Cuisinart bread pan back to the Cuisinart Bread Machine
6. Close the lid and Select program: white.
7. Select Crust color: medium and Loaf size;1 1/2-lb press the start button
8. Remove bread and allow to cool; serve, and enjoy.

Serving Suggestion: Serve with chicken spinach dip

Preparation and Cooking Tips: ingredients must be at room temperature

Olive Ham Bread

The little Italian bread will leave you wanting more, well-spiced, and delicious. One of those lovely Mediterranean loaves that serve as lunch.

Prep time: 5 minutes

Cooking time: 3hours 25minutes

Serves: 1 Loaf

Ingredients To Use:

Dry ingredients

- 2 cup of wheat flour
- 1 tsp black pepper
- 2 tsp. Baking powder
- 1 tsp mixed spice
- 1 tsp of salt

Wet ingredients

- 2 tbsp. olive oil
- 1 ham, finely chopped
- ½ cup of cheddar cheese, grated
- 2/3 cup of black olives, pitted
- ½ cup of milk
- 3 eggs, whisked

Step-by-Step Directions to Cook It:

1. Mix milk, egg, oil in a bowl, stir in the rest of the wet ingredients
2. Mix flour, baking powder, spice, salt, and black pepper in a bowl
3. Pour the liquid ingredients into the Cuisinart bread pan, then the Dry ingredients
4. insert Cuisinart bread pan back to the Cuisinart Bread Machine
5. Close the lid and Select program: white.
6. Select Crust color: medium and Loaf size; 1 ½ -lb press the start button
7. Remove bread and allow to cool; serve, and enjoy.

Serving Suggestion: serve with balsamic days

Preparation and Cooking Tips: egg must be at room temperature

Bacon, Cheese, and Jalapeno Bread

This bread has it all, creamy cheese, spicy jalapeno, and crispy bacon. The bread makes a great sandwich

Prep time: 5 minutes

Cooking time: 3hours 25minutes

Serves: 1 Loaf

Ingredients To Use:

Dry ingredients

- 3 cup of wheat flour
- 1 tsp black pepper
- 1 tsp. Baking powder
- 2 tsp sugar
- 1 tsp of salt

Wet ingredients

- 2 jalapeno, chopped
- 3 bacon, finely chopped
- 2 cup of cheddar cheese, grated
- 2 scallions, chopped
- 1 egg, whisked
- 1 ½ cup of milk
- 1 tbsp melted butter

Step-by-Step Directions to Cook It:

1. Mix flour, salt, sugar, baking powder, and black pepper
2. Mix egg, butter, and milk in a bowl
3. Stir in the remaining ingredients
4. Pour the liquid ingredients into the Cuisinart bread pan, then the Dry ingredients
5. insert Cuisinart bread pan back to the Cuisinart Bread Machine
6. Close the lid and Select program: white.
7. Select Crust color: medium and Loaf size;1 1/2-lb.
8. Press the start button
9. Remove bread and allow to cool; serve, and enjoy.

Serving Suggestion: Use to prepare a chicken sandwich

Preparation and Cooking Tips: egg must be at room temperature

Bacon and Cheese Bread

One quality that will endear you to this bread is the aroma but wait until you taste this piece of heaven

Prep time: 5 minutes

Cooking time: 3hours 25minutes

Serves: 1 Loaf

Ingredients To Use:

Dry ingredients

- 4 cup of wheat flour
- 2 tsp. yeast
- 1 tsp of salt

Wet ingredients

- 2 tbsp. Butter
- 1 cup of bacon, crumbled
- 2 cup of romano cheese
- 1 cup of milk
- 3 eggs, whisked

Step-by-Step Directions to Cook It:

1. Mix egg, milk, and butter in a bowl. Stir in the cheese and bacon
2. Mix flour and salt in a bowl.
3. Pour the liquid ingredients into the Cuisinart bread pan, then the Dry ingredients
4. Make a shallow well in the center and add the yeast
5. insert Cuisinart bread pan back to the Cuisinart Bread Machine
6. Close the lid and Select program: white.
7. Select Crust color: medium and Loaf size; 1 1/2-lb.
8. Press the start button
9. Remove bread and allow to cool; serve, and enjoy.

Serving Suggestion: serve with jam

Preparation and Cooking Tips: egg mist be at room temperature

Olive Bacon Bread

This golden dough is so puffy and tasty: Also, it is good with several side dishes. Try it out and enjoy

Prep time: 5 minutes

Cooking time: 3hours 25 minutes

Serves: 1 Loaf

Ingredients To Use:

Dry ingredients

- 2 cup of wheat flour
- 1 tsp granulated sugar
- 2 tsp. Baking powder
- 1 cup of bread flour
- 1 tsp of salt

Wet ingredients

- 3 slices of ham, chopped
- 2 1/2 tbsp. olive oil
- 1 ¼ cup of warm water
- 1 ham, finely chopped
- ½ cup of cheddar cheese, grated
- 2/3 cup of black olives, pitted
- ½ cup of milk
- 4 eggs, whisked

Step-by-Step Directions to Cook It:

1. Mix egg, water, milk, and oil in a bowl. Stir in the remaining wet ingredients
2. Mix flour, sugar, salt, baking powder, and wheat flour in a bowl.
3. Pour the liquid ingredients into the Cuisinart bread pan; then the Dry ingredients
4. insert Cuisinart bread pan back to the Cuisinart Bread Machine
5. Close the lid and Select program: white.
6. Select Crust color: medium and Loaf size; 1 ½ -lb.
7. Press the start button
8. Remove bread and allow to cool; serve, and enjoy.

Serving Suggestion: serve with butter

Preparation and Cooking Tips: eggs must be at room temperature

Tomato and Chorizo Bread

The chorizo tomato bread is spicy and colorful; you are simply going to love it.

Prep time: 5 minutes

Cooking time: 3 hours 5minutes

Serves: 1 Loaf

Ingredients To Use:

Dry ingredients

- 2 cup of wheat flour
- 2 tbsp granulated sugar
- 2 tsp. Active dry yeast
- ¼ cup of chorizo sausage, diced
- 1 cup of bread flour
- 1 tsp. Smoked paprika
- 3 tbsp. Onion flakes
- 1 tsp of salt

Wet ingredients

- 3 tbsp tomato puree
- 2 1/2 tbsp. olive oil
- 1 ¼ cup of warm water

Step-by-Step Directions to Cook It:

1. Add the tomato puree, oil, and water to a bowl, stir
2. Add dry ingredients except for the yeast in a bowl
3. Pour the liquid ingredients into the Cuisinart bread pan, then the Dry ingredients
4. Make a shallow well in the center and add the yeast
5. insert Cuisinart bread pan back to the Cuisinart Bread Machine
6. Close the lid and Select program: white.
7. Select Crust color: medium and Loaf size; 1 1/2-lb, press the start button
8. Remove bread and allow to cool; serve, and enjoy.

Serving Suggestion: serve with any dippings

Preparation and Cooking Tips: all the dry ingredient to be well incorporated

CHAPTER 10: POULTRY BREAD

Whole Wheat Chicken Bread

Whole wheat chicken bread is simply delicious and satisfying. Using the Cuisinart bread maker makes it easy to prepare this bread

Prep time: 5 minutes
Cooking time: 3hours 25 minutes
Serves: 1 Loaf

Ingredients To Use:

Dry Ingredients

- 2 cups of Whole wheat flour
- 1 tsp Yeast
- 1/4 tsp Salt
- 2 tsp Sugar

Wet Ingredients

- 2 Tbsp Olive oil
- 1 tsp Vinegar
- 4 Tbsp. Yogurt
- 2 tbsp Butter
- 1 cup of Milk
- 1/2 tsp Mustard paste

Chicken Filling

- ½ lb. Chicken, shredded
- 2 tbsp. Flour
- 1/2 cup of Spring onions
- 1/2 tsp Salt
- 1/2 cup of Carrots, shredded
- 3 tbsp. Tikka masala
- 1 tsp Black pepper

Step-by-Step Directions to Cook It:

1. Mix all the filling ingredients in a bowl, cover and set aside
2. Mix sugar, salt, and flour in a bowl
3. Mix all the wet ingredients in another bowl
4. Pour the liquid ingredients into the Cuisinart bread pan, then the Dry ingredients
5. Make a shallow well in the center and add the yeast
6. insert Cuisinart bread pan back to the Cuisinart Bread Machine
7. Close the lid and Select program; white.
8. Select Crust color: medium and Loaf size;1 1/2-lb. Press the start button
9. After the knead process, press pause and remove the bread. Roll-out on a flat surface. Add the chicken filling and shape it into a ball.
10. Return to the Cuisinart Bread pan and press start to resume the program.
11. Remove bread and allow to cool; serve, and enjoy.

Serving Suggestion: Serve with sauce of choice

Preparation and Cooking Tips: you can cook the chicken filling

Chicken Bread

This is another creative way of preparing chicken Bread; enjoy the chicken's succulent and chewy taste in this bread.

Prep time: 5 minutes

Cooking time: 3hours 25 minutes

Serves: 1 Loaf

Ingredients To Use:

Dry Ingredients

- 3 cups of Flour
- 1 Cup of Sugar
- 1 Tsp Salt
- 2 Tbsps Yeast

Wet Ingredients

- 1 Apple Cider Vinegar
- 3 Tbsps Butter
- 1 Cup of Water
- 1 Cup of Milk
- 2 Eggs, whisked

For the Chicken Filling:

- 1/2 lb boiled boneless chicken, shredded
- 1 Green Pepper, sliced
- 2 medium-size tomatoes, chopped
- 1 Red bell pepper, sliced
- 1 Bulb of Onion
- 2 tsp. Ginger powder
- 1 Tsp Curry powder
- 1/4 Cup of Flour
- Salt and Black pepper to taste

Step-by-Step Directions to Cook It:

1. Mix the fillings in a bowl, set aside.
2. Mix flour, sugar, and salt in a bowl
3. Add vinegar, water, butter, milk, and egg in another bowl.
4. Pour the liquid ingredients into the Cuisinart bread pan, then the Dry ingredients
5. Make a shallow well in the center and add the yeast
6. insert Cuisinart bread pan back to the Cuisinart Bread Machine
7. Close the lid and Select program: white.
8. Select Crust color: medium and Loaf size:1 1/2-lb. Press the start button
9. Remove the dough after the kneading process; roll-out and add the chicken filling.
10. Reshape and return to the Cuisinart Bread Maker, press start to resume program.
11. Remove bread and allow to cool; serve, and enjoy.

Serving Suggestion: Serve with any sauce of choice

Preparation and Cooking Tips: allow the chicken to marinate

Braided Chicken Bread

Braided chicken bread is moist, tasty, and the chicken is tender and juicy. Besides, it has an excellent presentation

Prep time: 5 minutes
Cooking time: 3hours 25 minutes
Serves: 1 Loaf

Ingredients To Use:

Dry Ingredients

- 4 cups of all-purpose flour
- 1 tbsp instant yeast
- 1 tsp salt
- 1 tsp granulated sugar

Wet ingredients

- 1/2 cup of warm water
- 2 tbsps butter, melted
- 1/2 cup of milk
- 2 eggs, whisked

For the Chicken Filling

- 2 cups of boiled and shredded chicken
- 2 medium red onions, chopped
- 1 tsp salt
- 1 tsp crushed black pepper
- 4 tbsp fresh coriander, chopped

Step-by-Step Directions to Cook It:

1. Mix the chicken filling in a bowl and set aside
2. Mix flour, salt, and sugar in a bowl
3. Mix water, milk, butter, and egg in another bowl
4. Pour the liquid ingredients into the Cuisinart bread pan, then the Dry ingredients
5. Make a shallow well in the center and add the yeast
6. insert Cuisinart bread pan back to the Cuisinart Bread Machine
7. Close the lid and Select program: white.
8. Select Crust color: medium and Loaf size;1 1/2-lb press the start button
9. After the kneading process, remove from the Cuisinart bread pan.
10. Remove the dough after the kneading process; roll-out and add the chicken filling.
11. Reshape and return to the Cuisinart Bread Maker, press start to resume program
12. Remove and allow to cool, serve, and enjoy

Serving Suggestion: serve with salad and sauce

Preparation and Cooking Tips: allow the chicken to marinate

Chicken Parmesan Loaf

Enjoy the delicious and cheesy taste of this bread with salad and sauce of choice; so yummy.

Prep time: 5 minutes
Cooking time: 3 hours 25 minutes
Serves: 1 Loaf

Ingredients To Use:

Dry Ingredients

- 4 cups of all-purpose flour
- 1 tbsp instant yeast
- 1 tsp salt
- 1 tsp granulated sugar

Wet ingredients

- 2 tbsp butter, melted
- 2 eggs, whisked
- ½ cup of grated Parmesan cheese
- 1 cup of warm water
- ½ cup of tomato sauce
- ½ cup of grated provolone cheese
- 1 tbsp olive oil

For the Chicken Filling

- 2 cups of boiled and shredded chicken
- 2 medium red onions, chopped
- 1 tsp salt
- 1 tsp crushed black pepper

Step-by-Step Directions to Cook It:

1. Mix the chicken filling in a bowl and set aside
2. Mix flour, salt, and sugar in a bowl
3. Mix all the wet ingredients in a bowl.
4. Pour the liquid ingredients into the Cuisinart bread pan, then the Dry ingredients
5. Make a shallow well in the center and add the yeast
6. insert Cuisinart bread pan back to the Cuisinart Bread Machine
7. Close the lid and Select program: white.
8. Select Crust color: medium and Loaf size;1 1/2-lb press the start button
9. After the kneading process, remove from the Cuisinart bread pan.
10. Remove the dough after the kneading process; roll-out and add the chicken filling.
11. Reshape and return to the Cuisinart Bread Maker, press start to resume program
12. Remove and allow to cool, serve, and enjoy

Serving Suggestion: serve with salad

Preparation and Cooking Tips: allow the chicken to marinate

Whole-wheat Turkey Bread

Whole wheat turkey bread tastes just as delicious as the chicken bread. Get creative with leftover turkey from Thanksgiving.

Prep time: 5 minutes
Cooking time: 3 hours 5 minutes
Serves: 1 Loaf

Ingredients To Use:

Dry Ingredients

- 2 cups of Whole wheat flour
- 1 tsp Yeast
- 1/4 tsp Salt
- 2 tsp Sugar

Wet Ingredients

- 2 tbsp Olive oil
- 1 tsp Vinegar
- 4 Tbsp. Yogurt
- 2 tbsp Butter
- 1 cup of Milk
- 1/2 tsp Mustard paste

Turkey Filling

- ½ lb Turkey, shredded
- 2 tbsp. Flour
- 1/2 cup of Spring onions
- 1/2 tsp Salt
- 1/2 cup of Carrots shredded
- 3 tbsp. Tikka masala
- 1 tsp Black pepper

Step-by-Step Directions to Cook It:

1. Mix all the filling ingredients in a bowl, cover and set aside
2. Mix sugar, salt, and flour in a bowl
3. Mix all the wet ingredients in another bowl
4. Pour the liquid ingredients into the Cuisinart bread pan, then the Dry ingredients
5. Make a shallow well in the center and add the yeast
6. insert Cuisinart bread pan back to the Cuisinart Bread Machine
7. Close the lid and Select program; white.
8. Select Crust color: medium and Loaf size;1 1/2-lb. Press the start button
9. After the knead process, press pause and remove the bread. Roll-out on a flat surface. Add the filling and shape into a ball.
10. Return to the Cuisinart Bread pan and press start to resume the program.
11. Remove bread and allow to cool; serve, and enjoy.

Serving Suggestion:serve with salad

Preparation and Cooking Tips: allow the meat to marinate

Braided Turkey Bread

Braided turkey bread is a moist and tender bread that is made easier to prepare with the Cuisinart bread maker

Prep time: 5 minutes
Cooking time:
Serves: 1 Loaf

Ingredients To Use:

Dry Ingredients

- 4 cups of all-purpose flour
- 1 tbsp instant yeast
- 1 tsp salt
- 1 tsp granulated sugar

Wet ingredients

- 1/2 cup of warm water
- 2 tbsps butter, melted
- 1/2 cup of milk
- 2 eggs, whisked

For the turkey Filling

- 2 cups of boiled and shredded turkey
- 2 medium red onions, chopped
- 1 tsp salt
- 1 tsp crushed black pepper
- 4 tbsp fresh coriander, chopped

Step-by-Step Directions to Cook It:

1. Mix the turkey filling in a bowl and set aside
2. Mix flour, salt, and sugar in a bowl
3. Mix water, milk, butter, and egg in another bowl
4. Pour the liquid ingredients into the Cuisinart bread pan, then the Dry ingredients
5. Make a shallow well in the center and add the yeast
6. insert Cuisinart bread pan back to the Cuisinart Bread Machine
7. Close the lid and Select program: white.
8. Select Crust color: medium and Loaf size;1 1/2-lb press the start button
9. After the kneading process, remove from the Cuisinart bread pan.
10. Remove the dough after the kneading process; roll-out and add the filling.
11. Reshape and return to the Cuisinart Bread Maker, press start to resume program
12. Remove and allow to cool, serve, and enjoy

Serving Suggestion: Serve with any sauce of choice

Preparation and Cooking Tips: ingredients must be at room temperature

Turkey light Roll

Here is a recipe to lighten up the mood on Thanksgiving day. They are small, delicious, and tasty. Serve with any sauce of choice

Prep time: 5 minutes

Cooking time: 3 hours 25 minutes

Serves: 1 Loaf

Ingredients To Use:

Dry Ingredients

- 4 cups of all-purpose flour
- 1 tbsp instant yeast
- 1 tsp salt
- 1 tsp granulated sugar

Wet ingredients

- 1/2 cup of warm water
- 2 tbsps butter, melted
- 1/2 cup of milk
- 2 eggs, whisked

For the turkey Filling

- 2 cups of boiled and shredded turkey
- ½ cup of. Chopped bacon
- 1 tsp salt
- 1 tsp crushed black pepper

Step-by-Step Directions to Cook It:

1. Mix the turkey filling in a bowl and set aside
2. Mix flour, salt, and sugar in a bowl
3. Mix water, milk, butter, and egg in another bowl
4. Pour the liquid ingredients into the Cuisinart bread pan, then the Dry ingredients
5. Make a shallow well in the center and add the yeast
6. insert Cuisinart bread pan back to the Cuisinart Bread Machine
7. Close the lid and Select program: white.
8. Select Crust color: medium and Loaf size;1 1/2-lb press the start button
9. After the kneading process, remove from the Cuisinart bread pan.
10. Remove the dough after the kneading process; roll-out and add the filling.
11. Reshape and return to the Cuisinart Bread Maker, press start to resume program
12. Remove and allow to cool, serve, and enjoy

Serving Suggestion Serve with salad

Preparation and Cooking Tips: season the filling to taste

Chicken Fish Bread

The chicken fish bread is so delicious; it can easily turn into your favorite lunch meal. Enjoy with a nice topping.

Prep time: 5 minutes

Cooking time: 3hours 5 minutes

Serves: 1 Loaf

Ingredients To Use:

Dry Ingredients

- 3 cups of Flour
- 1 Cup of Sugar
- 1 Tsp Salt
- 2 Tbsps Yeast

Wet Ingredients

- 1 Apple Cider Vinegar
- 3 Tbsps Butter
- 1 Cup of Water
- 1 Cup of Milk
- 2 Eggs, whisked

For the Chicken Filling:

- 1/2 lb boiled boneless chicken, shredded
- 1 Green Pepper, sliced
- 2 medium-size tomatoes, chopped
- 1 Red bell pepper, sliced
- 1 Bulb of Onion
- 2 tsp. Ginger powder
- 1 Tsp Curry powder
- 1/4 Cup of fish, shredded
- Salt and Black pepper to taste

Step-by-Step Directions to Cook It:

1. Mix the fillings in a bowl, set aside.
2. Mix flour, sugar, and salt in a bowl
3. Add vinegar, water, butter, milk, and egg in another bowl.
4. Pour the liquid ingredients into the Cuisinart bread pan, then the Dry ingredients

5. Make a shallow well in the center and add the yeast
6. insert Cuisinart bread pan back to the Cuisinart Bread Machine
7. Close the lid and Select program: white.
8. Select Crust color: medium and Loaf size:1 1/2-lb. Press the start button
9. Remove the dough after the kneading process; roll-out and add the chicken filling.
10. Reshape and return to the Cuisinart Bread Maker, press start to resume program.
11. Remove bread and allow to cool; serve, and enjoy.

Serving Suggestion: Serve with any sauce of choice

Preparation and Cooking Tips: season the filling to taste

CHAPTER 11: SEAFOOD BREAD

Craw Fish Bread

The crawfish bread has a lot; the aroma, taste, and flavor are so enticing. It is highly nutritious

Prep time: 5 minutes
Cooking time: 3 hours 5 minutes
Serves: 1 Loaf

Ingredients To Use:

Dry Ingredients

- 2 cups of Whole wheat flour
- 1 tsp Yeast
- 1/4 tsp Salt
- 2 tsp Sugar

Wet Ingredients

- 2 tbsp Olive oil
- 1 tsp Vinegar
- 4 Tbsp. Yogurt
- 2 tbsp Butter
- 1 cup of Milk
- 1/2 tsp Mustard paste

Filling

- 1 cup of crawfish, minced
- 2 tbsp. Flour
- 1/2 cup of Spring onions
- 1/2 tsp Salt
- 1 tsp Black pepper

Step-by-Step Directions to Cook It:

1. Mix all the filling ingredients in a bowl, cover and set aside
2. Mix sugar, salt, and flour in a bowl
3. Mix all the wet ingredients in another bowl
4. Pour the liquid ingredients into the Cuisinart bread pan, then the Dry ingredients
5. Make a shallow well in the center and add the yeast
6. insert Cuisinart bread pan back to the Cuisinart Bread Machine
7. Close the lid and Select program; white.
8. Select Crust color: medium and Loaf size;1 1/2-lb. Press the start button
9. After the knead process, press pause and remove the bread. Roll-out on a flat surface. Add the filling and shape into a ball.
10. Return to the Cuisinart Bread pan and press start to resume the program.
11. Remove bread and allow to cool; serve, and enjoy.

Serving Suggestion: Serve with sauce of choice

Preparation and Cooking Tips: leave ingredients to marinate for a few minutes

Fish Pizza Bread

Recreate the pizza dough and fillings with this recipe, simple and easy to prepare. The filling enriches the taste of the dough.

Prep time: 5 minutes
Cooking time: 3hours 25minutes
Serves: 1 Loaf

Ingredients To Use:

Dry Ingredients

- 2 cups of bread flour
- 1 tsp Yeast
- 1/4 tsp Salt
- 1/2 tsp Sugar

Wet Ingredients

- 1 tbsp Olive oil
- 1 cup of Milk
- 2 Eggs, whisked

Filling

- 1 tbsp. Pizza sauce
- ½ cup of shredded fish
- 1 tbsp. Yogurt
- 1 tsp. Tikka masala

Step-by-Step Directions to Cook It:

1. Mix the filling in a bowl and set aside
2. Mix flour, salt, and sugar in a bowl
3. Mix milk, oil, and egg in another bowl
4. Pour the liquid ingredients into the Cuisinart bread pan, then the Dry ingredients
5. Make a shallow well in the center and add the yeast
6. insert Cuisinart bread pan back to the Cuisinart Bread Machine
7. Close the lid and Select program: white.
8. Select Crust color: medium and Loaf size;1 1/2-lb press the start button
9. After the kneading process, remove from the Cuisinart bread pan.
10. Remove the dough after the kneading process; roll-out and add the filling.
11. Reshape and return to the Cuisinart Bread Maker, press start to resume program
12. Remove and allow to cool, serve, and enjoy

Serving Suggestion: serve garnished with cheese

Preparation and Cooking Tips: use any fish of choice

Shrimp Bread

Enjoy the rich taste of the shrimp in this tender and moist bread loaf. The flavor is unique and mouthwatering

Prep time: 5 minutes

Cooking time: 3hours 5 minutes

Serves: 1 Loaf

Ingredients To Use:

Dry Ingredients

- 2 cups of Whole wheat flour
- 1 tsp Yeast
- 1/4 tsp Salt
- 2 tsp Sugar

Wet Ingredients

- 2 tbsp Olive oil
- 1 tsp Vinegar
- 2 tbsp Butter
- 1 cup of Milk

Filling

- 1 cup of shrimp, minced
- 2 tbsp. Flour
- 1/2 cup of Spring onions
- 1/2 tsp Salt
- 1 tsp Black pepper

Step-by-Step Directions to Cook It:

1. Mix all the filling ingredients in a bowl, cover and set aside
2. Mix sugar, salt, and flour in a bowl
3. Mix all the wet ingredients in another bowl
4. Pour the liquid ingredients into the Cuisinart bread pan, then the Dry ingredients
5. Make a shallow well in the center and add the yeast
6. insert Cuisinart bread pan back to the Cuisinart Bread Machine
7. Close the lid and Select program; white.
8. Select Crust color: medium and Loaf size;1 1/2-lb. Press the start button
9. After the knead process, press pause and remove the bread. Roll-out on a flat surface. Add the filling and shape into a ball.
10. Return to the Cuisinart Bread pan and press start to resume the program.
11. Remove bread and allow to cool; serve, and enjoy.

Serving Suggestion: Serve as an appetizer

Preparation and Cooking Tips: leave fish to marinate for a few minutes

Seafood Bread

Who says you can get creative with those crabs and shrimp. Incorporate it into your bread, and you have a piece of heaven.

Prep time: 5 minutes

Cooking time: 3hours 25minutes

Serves: 1 Loaf

Ingredients To Use:

Dry Ingredients

- 2 cups of Whole wheat flour
- 1 tsp Yeast
- 1/4 tsp Salt
- 2 tsp Sugar

Wet Ingredients

- 2 tbsp Olive oil
- 1 tsp Vinegar
- 2 tbsp Butter
- 1 cup of Milk

Filling

- 1 cup of shrimp, minced
- 1 cup of crab meat, minced
- 2 tbsp. Apple cider vinegar
- 1/2 cup of Spring onions
- 1/2 tsp Salt
- 1 tsp Black pepper

Step-by-Step Directions to Cook It:

1. Mix all the filling ingredients in a bowl, cover and set aside
2. Mix sugar, salt, and flour in a bowl
3. Mix all the wet ingredients in another bowl
4. Pour the liquid ingredients into the Cuisinart bread pan, then the Dry ingredients
5. Make a shallow well in the center and add the yeast
6. insert Cuisinart bread pan back to the Cuisinart Bread Machine
7. Close the lid and Select program; white.
8. Select Crust color: medium and Loaf size;1 1/2-lb. Press the start button
9. After the knead process, press pause and remove the bread. Roll-out on a flat surface. Add the filling and shape into a ball.
10. Return to the Cuisinart Bread pan and press start to resume the program.
11. Remove bread and allow to cool; serve, and enjoy.

Serving Suggestion: Serve with sauce of choice

Preparation and Cooking Tips: leave the meat to marinate

Fish Bread Roll

The fish bread roll is a savory and delicious snack that will leave you wanting more. Serve with cold juice.

Prep time: 5 minutes

Cooking time: 3hours 25 minutes.

Serves: 1 Loaf

Ingredients To Use:

Dry Ingredients

- 2 cups of Whole wheat flour
- 1 tsp Yeast
- 1/4 tsp Salt
- 2 tsp Sugar

Wet Ingredients

- 2 tbsp Olive oil
- 1 tsp Vinegar
- 2 tbsp Butter
- 1 cup of Milk

Filling

- 1 cup of fish, shredded
- 1 tbsp. Chili powder
- Salt to taste
- 2 tsp ginger-garlic paste
- 1/2 tsp Salt
- 1 tsp Black pepper

Step-by-Step Directions to Cook It:

1. Mix all the filling ingredients in a bowl, cover and set aside
2. Mix sugar, salt, and flour in a bowl
3. Mix all the wet ingredients in another bowl
4. Pour the liquid ingredients into the Cuisinart bread pan, then the Dry ingredients
5. Make a shallow well in the center and add the yeast
6. insert Cuisinart bread pan back to the Cuisinart Bread Machine
7. Close the lid and Select program; white.
8. Select Crust color: medium and Loaf size;1 1/2-lb. Press the start button
9. After the knead process, press pause and remove the bread. Roll-out on a flat surface. Add the filling and shape into a ball.
10. Return to the Cuisinart Bread pan and press start to resume the program.
11. Remove bread and allow to cool; serve, and enjoy.

Serving Suggestion: serve with mint chutney

Preparation and Cooking Tips: allow the fish to marinate

Parmesan Cheese and Shrimp Bread

The parmesan cheese and shrimp bread are cheesy and delicious with a unique flavor. Enjoy for lunch.

Prep time: 5 minutes

Cooking time: 3hours 5minutes

Serves: 1 Loaf

Ingredients To Use:

Dry ingredients

- 1 ¼ cup of wheat flour
- 2 tsp baking powder
- 2 tsp. Active dry yeast.
- 1/2 tsp baking soda
- 1 cup of bread flour
- 1 tsp of salt

Wet ingredients

- 1 cup of shrimp, minced
- 2 eggs
- 2 1/2 tbsp. olive oil
- ¼ cup of shredded parmesan cheese
- 1 ¼ cups of buttermilk

Step-by-Step Directions to Cook It:

1. Mix oil, parmesan cheese, and buttermilk.
2. Mix all the dry ingredients in a pan except the yeast
3. Pour the wet ingredients into the Cuisinart bread pan, then the Dry ingredients
4. Make a shallow well in the center and add the yeast
5. insert Cuisinart bread pan back to the Cuisinart Bread Machine
6. Close the lid and Select program; Whole Wheat.
7. Select Crust color: medium and Loaf size;1 ½-lb press the start button
8. After the kneading process, add the shrimp.
9. Press start to resume the program.
10. Remove bread and allow to cool; serve, and enjoy.

Serving Suggestion: Serve with sauce

Preparation and Cooking Tips: Add more water if the dough is too dry.

Bacon, Cheddar, and Crab Bread

The bacon, cheddar, and crab bread is the ultimate combo; you are going to love preparing this recipe

Prep time: 5 minutes

Cooking time: 3 hours 25 minutes

Serves: 1 Loaf

Ingredients To Use:

Dry ingredients

- 1 ¼ cup of wheat flour
- 2 tsp baking powder
- 2 tsp. Active dry yeast.
- 1/2 tsp baking soda
- 1 cup of bread flour
- 1 tsp of salt

Wet ingredients

- 1 cup of crab meat, minced
- 5 bacon slice, chopped
- 2 eggs
- 2 1/2 tbsp. olive oil
- ¼ cup of shredded parmesan cheese
- 1 ¼ cups of buttermilk

Step-by-Step Directions to Cook It:

1. Mix oil, parmesan cheese, and buttermilk. Stir in the bacon.
2. Mix all the dry ingredients in a pan except the yeast
3. Pour the wet ingredients into the Cuisinart bread pan, then the Dry ingredients
4. Make a shallow well in the center and add the yeast
5. insert Cuisinart bread pan back to the Cuisinart Bread Machine
6. Close the lid and Select program; Whole Wheat.
7. Select Crust color: medium and Loaf size;1 ½-lb press the start button
8. After the kneading process, add the shrimp. Press start to resume the program.
9. Remove bread and allow to cool; serve, and enjoy.

Serving Suggestion: Serve with any sauce of choice

Preparation and Cooking Tips: add more flour if the dough is too wet

Shrimp and Bacon Bread

The combination of shrimps and bacon creates a unique flavor that is simply enticing. Enjoy for lunch!

Prep time: 5 minutes

Cooking time:

Serves: 1 Loaf

Ingredients To Use:

Dry ingredients

- 1 ¼ cup of wheat flour
- 2 tsp baking powder
- 2 tsp. Active dry yeast.
- 1/2 tsp baking soda
- 1 cup of bread flour
- 1 tsp of salt

Wet ingredients

- 7 crispy bacon strips chopped
- 2 eggs
- 2 1/2 tbsp. olive oil
- 1 cup of shrimp, minced
- 1 ¼ cups of buttermilk

Step-by-Step Directions to Cook It:

1. Mix eggs, oil, cheese, buttermilk in a pan, add the bacon, and mix.
2. Mix wheat flour, baking powder, bread flour, and salt in a bowl
3. Pour the wet ingredients into the Cuisinart bread pan, then the Dry ingredients
4. Make a shallow well in the center and add the yeast
5. insert Cuisinart bread pan back to the Cuisinart Bread Machine
6. Close the lid and Select program: white.
7. Select Crust color: medium and Loaf size;1 1/2-lb press the start button
8. Add the shrimps after the kneading process, press start to continue the program
9. Remove bread and allow to cool; serve, and enjoy.

Serving Suggestion: serve with salad

Preparation and Cooking Tips: add water if the dough is too dry

CHAPTER 12: GLUTEN-FREE BREAD

Gluten-Free Seed and Nut Bread

This is a classic gluten-free recipe that is delicious; it is well spiced and full of flavors. Even gluten eaters are going to love this recipe.

Prep time: 5 minutes

Cooking time: 2 hours 15 minutes

Serves: 1 Loaf

Ingredients To Use:

Dry ingredients

- 2 ½ cup of gluten-free multipurpose flour
- ½ cup of milk powder
- 2 ¼ tsp active dry yeast
- 1 tbsp xanthan gum
- ¼ cup of sesame seeds
- ¼ cup of chopped walnuts
- ¼ cup of sunflower seeds
- ¼ cup of cornstarch
- ¼ cup of flax seeds
- 1 tsp kosher salt

Wet ingredients

- 3 eggs
- 1 ¼ cups of water
- 2 tbsp unsalted butter

Step-by-Step Directions to Cook It:

1. Mix egg, butter, and water in a bowl.
2. Mix the dry ingredients in a bowl except for the yeast.
3. Pour the liquid ingredients into the Cuisinart bread pan, then the Dry ingredients
4. Make a shallow well in the center and add the yeast
5. insert Cuisinart bread pan back to the Cuisinart Bread Machine
6. Close the lid and Select program; Gluten-free.
7. Select Crust color; Medium and Loaf size;1 ½-lb. press the start button
8. Remove bread and allow to cool; serve, and enjoy.

Serving Suggestion: serve with scrambled egg

Preparation and Cooking Tips: all ingredients must be at room temperature

Gluten-free Fruit Bread

The gluten-free fruit bread is filled with different fruits that contribute to the flavor of the bread. Better enjoy with toppings and sauce.

Prep time: 5 minutes

Cooking time: 2hours 15 minutes

Serves: 1 Loaf

Ingredients To Use:

Dry ingredients

- 1 cup of potato flour
- 1 cup of brown rice flour
- 1½ tsp active dried yeast
- ⅔ cup of buckwheat flour
- ½ cup of plus 1 tbsp coarse cornmeal
- 1 tsp ground cinnamon
- ½ cup of currants
- 1 tsp ground ginger
- ½ cup of golden raisins
- grated zest of 1 orange
- grated zest of 1 lemon
- a pinch of ground cloves
- 2 tsp salt

Wet ingredients

- 1¼ cups of warm water
- 2 tsp honey

Step-by-Step Directions to Cook It:

1. Mix warm water and honey in a bowl
2. Add all the dry ingredients in a bowl except the yeast
3. Pour the liquid ingredients into the Cuisinart bread pan, then the Dry ingredients
4. Make a shallow well in the center and add the yeast
5. insert Cuisinart bread pan back to the Cuisinart Bread Machine
6. Close the lid and Select program; Gluten-free.
7. Select Crust color; medium and Loaf size;1 ½-lb. press the start button
8. Remove bread and allow to cool; serve, and enjoy.

Serving Suggestion: serve with Jam

Preparation and Cooking Tips: all ingredients must be at room temperature

Gluten-free Classic Bread

The classic bread is another way of making gluten-free bread. There is elegance in the simplicity of this bread without any add-in.

Prep time: 5 minutes

Cooking time: 2 hours 15 minutes

Serves: 1 Loaf

Ingredients To Use:

Dry ingredients:

- 1 cup of potato flour
- 2¼ tsp active dry yeast
- ½ cup of plus 1 tbsp buckwheat flour
- 1 cup of brown rice flour
- ½ cup of plus 1 tbsp coarse cornmeal
- 2 tsp salt

Wet ingredients

- 1½ cups of warm water

Step-by-Step Directions to Cook It:

1. Mix all the dry ingredients in a bowl except the yeast
2. Pour the liquid ingredients into the Cuisinart bread pan, then the Dry ingredients
3. Make a shallow well in the center and add the yeast
4. insert Cuisinart bread pan back to the Cuisinart Bread Machine
5. Close the lid and Select program; Gluten-free.
6. Select Crust color; medium and Loaf size;1 ½-lb press the start button
7. Remove bread and allow to cool; serve, and enjoy.

Serving Suggestion: Serve with sauce of choice

Preparation and Cooking Tips: all ingredients must be at room temperature

Gluten-free Seeded Bread

This is a rich meal for the gluten intolerant populations. It is high in nutrients and can be served with several toppings.

Prep time: 5 minutes

Cooking time: 2 hours 15 minutes

Serves: 1 Loaf

Ingredients To Use:

Dry ingredients

- ⅔ cup of potato flour
- 1 cup of buckwheat flakes
- ⅔ cup of brown rice flour
- ⅓ cup of buckwheat flour
- ⅓ cup of sunflower seeds
- 1½ tsp active dried yeast
- ⅓ cup of pumpkin seeds
- 2 tbsp sesame seeds
- ¼ cup of flaxseed
- 2 tbsp poppy seeds
- 2 tsp salt

Wet ingredients

- 1⅔ cups of warm water
- 1 scant tbsp blackstrap

Step-by-Step Directions to Cook It:

1. Mix warm water and blackstrap in a bowl
2. Add dry ingredients in a pan except for the yeast
3. Pour the liquid ingredients into the Cuisinart bread pan, then the Dry ingredients
4. Make a shallow well in the center and add the yeast
5. insert Cuisinart bread pan back to the Cuisinart Bread Machine
6. Close the lid and Select program; Gluten-free.
7. Select Crust color; medium and Loaf size;1 ½-lb press the start button
8. Remove bread and allow to cool; serve, and enjoy.

Serving Suggestion: serve with salad

Preparation and Cooking Tips: ingredients must be at room temperature

Gluten-free Corn Bread

You might have tried other variation of cornbread but this taste just as good as the other. If you are gluten intolerant and love cornbread, here is a recipe for you.

Prep time: 5 minutes

Cooking time: 2hours 15 minutes

Serves: 1 Loaf

Ingredients To Use:

Dry ingredients

- 1½ cups of cornmeal
- 1 tsp active dry yeast
- ⅓ cup of potato flour
- 1 tsp salt

Wet ingredients

- ¾ cup of plus 1 tbsp warm water
- ½cup of cooked corn kernels

Step-by-Step Directions to Cook It:

1. Mix water and corn kernels in a bowl
2. Mix cornmeal, potato flour, and salt in another bowl
3. Pour the liquid ingredients into the Cuisinart bread pan, then the Dry ingredients
4. Make a shallow well in the center and add the yeast
5. insert Cuisinart bread pan back to the Cuisinart Bread Machine
6. Close the lid and Select program: Gluten-free.
7. Select Crust color; medium and Loaf size;1 ½-lb. press the start button
8. Remove bread and allow to cool; serve, and enjoy.

Serving Suggestion: serve with stew

Preparation and Cooking Tips: you can use fresh, frozen, or canned corn kernel

Multi-grain Bread

The multigrain bread has lots of blended flavors that is equal to that of wheat bread. The blended flour gives it a unique texture, flavor, and color.

Prep time: 5 minutes

Cooking time: 2hours 15 minutes

Serves: 1 Loaf

Ingredients To Use:

Dry ingredients

- 1 cup of Light Flour Blend
- 1 cup of sorghum flour
- ½ millet flour
- ¼ amaranth flour
- 2 tbsp. active dry yeast
- ¼ cup of granulated sugar
- ¼ cup of flaxseed meal
- 1 tbsp baking powder
- ½ buttermilk powder
- 2 tsp xanthan gum
- 2 tsp salt salt

Wet ingredients

- 1 cup of plus 1 tbsp warm water
- 1 tbsp honey
- 3 large eggs, whisked
- 1 tsp apple cider vinegar
- ¼ cup of olive oil

Step-by-Step Directions to Cook It:

1. Mix all the wet ingredients in a bowl
2. Mix all the dry ingredients in a bowl except the yeast
3. Pour the liquid ingredients into the Cuisinart bread pan, then the Dry ingredients
4. Make a shallow well in the center and add the yeast
5. insert Cuisinart bread pan back to the Cuisinart Bread Machine
6. Close the lid and Select program: Gluten-free.
7. Select Crust color; medium and Loaf size;1 ½-lb press the start button
8. Remove bread and allow to cool; serve, and enjoy.

Serving Suggestion: used to prepare steak sandwich

Preparation and Cooking Tips: eggs must be at room temperature

Gluten-Free Brown Bread

The gluten-free brown bread is versatile and can be used in the preparation of many side dishes. Enjoy as french toast or with bread spread.

Prep time: 5 minutes

Cooking time: 3hour 15 minutes

Serves: 1 Loaf

Ingredients To Use:

Dry ingredients

- 2 cups of Light Flour Blend
- ¾ cups of sorghum flour
- ¼ cup of cornflour
- 1 tbsp active dry yeast
- 1 /4 cup of milk powder
- 2 tbsp. Granulated sugar
- 1 tbsp baking powder
- 2 tsp xanthan gum
- ½ cup of dried currants
- 1 ½ tsp. salt

Wet ingredients

- 1 cup of plus 1 tbsp. Warm water
- ¼ cup of olive oil
- ½ cup of molasses
- 2 large eggs, whisked
- 2 tsp apple cider vinegar

Step-by-Step Directions to Cook It:

1. Mix all the warm ingredients in a bowl
2. Mix all the dry ingredients in a bowl except the yeast
3. Pour the liquid ingredients into the Cuisinart bread pan, then the Dry ingredients
4. Make a shallow well in the center and add the yeast
5. insert Cuisinart bread pan back to the Cuisinart Bread Machine
6. Close the lid and Select the program; gluten-free.
7. Select Crust color; medium and Loaf size;1 ½-lb press the start button
8. Remove bread and allow to cool; serve, and enjoy.

Serving Suggestion: used to prepare sandwiches

Preparation and Cooking Tips: egg must be at room temperature

Buckwheat Bread

Buckwheat is naturally free from gluten, which makes the flour ideal for the preparation of gluten-free bread.

Prep time: 5 minutes

Cooking time:2 hours 15 minutes

Serves: 1 Loaf

Ingredients To Use:

Dry ingredients

- 2 cups of Light Flour Blend
- 1 cup of buckwheat flour
- 2 tbsp. active dry yeast
- 1 /2 cup of milk powder
- 1 tbsp baking powder
- ¼ cup of flaxseed meal
- 2 tsp xanthan gum
- 1 1 /2 tsp kosher or fine sea salt

Wet ingredients

- 1 cup of plus 2 tbsp. Warm water
- 2 tsp apple cider vinegar
- 3 large eggs, whisked
- 3 tbsp. olive oil

Step-by-Step Directions to Cook It:

1. Mix water with vinegar, eggs, and olive oil in a bowl
2. Mix all the dry ingredients in a bowl except yeast.
3. Pour the liquid ingredients into the Cuisinart bread pan, then the Dry ingredients
4. Make a shallow well in the center and add the yeast
5. insert Cuisinart bread pan back to the Cuisinart Bread Machine
6. Close the lid and Select program; Gluten-free.
7. Select Crust color; medium and Loaf size;1 ½-lb. press the start button
8. Remove bread and allow to cool; serve, and enjoy.

Serving Suggestion: serve as steak sandwich

Preparation and Cooking Tips: egg must be at room temperature

CHAPTER 13: CAKES

Cuisinart Coconut Cake

Coconut cake is a yummy dessert rich in flavor and can be enjoyed alongside other meals.

Preparation time: 30 minutes
Cooking time: 60minutes
Serves: 4

Ingredients To Use:

- 175g of plain flour
- 120g of sugar
- 2 eggs
- 75g of desiccated coconut
- 2 tsp of baking powder
- 125g of margarine
- 90ml of milk

Step-by-Step Directions to Cook It:

1. Whisk egg in a bowl and add sugar, coconut, and milk.
2. In another bowl, mix the flour, baking powder, and butter
3. Mix properly with your fingers until the mixture looks like bread crumbs.
4. Remove the paddle from the bread pan and put it in your egg mixture, after which, you add your flour mixture.
5. Sprinkle coconut on the mixture and fix the bread pan into the Cuisinart Bread Machine and cover the lid.
6. Select the start button and choose the bake program.
7. Set the timer for 50 minutes.
8. When the bread is done, bring it out to cool.

Serving suggestions: whipped cream can be used as toppings
Preparation and Cooking Tips: butter can be used in place of margarine

Panettone Cake

Panettone cake is a delicious bread usually prepared for Christmas and new year celebrations in Europe.

Preparation time:25 minutes

Cooking time: 1hour 45 minutes

Serves: 5

Ingredients To Use:

- 180ml of milk
- 130g of sugar
- 130g of butter
- 4 egg yolks
- 5g of salt
- 1 lemon
- 2 tsp of vanilla extract
- 130g of chocolate chips
- 1 packet of dry yeast
- 400g strong flour

Step-by-Step Directions to Cook It:

1. Put paddle at the bottom of the bread pan, pour in milk, butter, egg, salt, egg yolks, vanilla extract, lemon, strong flour, and yeast.
2. Insert bread pan into the Cuisinart Bread Machine and close lid.
3. Select the kneading and rising program and set the timer for 1hour,
4. After the kneading and rising cycle are complete, bring out the dough and place it on a flat surface.
5. Flatten the dough and sprinkle chocolate chips all over, after which, you fold back again.
6. Place the Molded dough back into the bread pan and insert into the Cuisinart Bread Machine
7. Select baking option for 50 minutes. Select the medium crust and 1½ lb loaf size.
8. When done, select the keep warm program for 15 minutes, then bring it out to cool.

Serving suggestions: top with whipped cream

Preparation and Cooking Tips: all-purpose flour can be used in place of strong white flour.

Lemon Pound Cake

Lemon pound cake is soft and tasty. It is rich in flavor, always moist with lemon taste.

Preparation time: 12 minutes

Cooking time: 55 minutes

Serves: 6

Ingredients To Use:

- ½ cup of butter
- 1 cup of white sugar
- 3 eggs
- 2 teaspoon of lemon zest
- 1 Tbsp of lemon juice
- 2 teaspoon of vanilla
- 1½ cups of all-purpose flour
- ¼ Tbsp of salt
- ¼ baking soda
- 1/3 sour cream

Step-by-Step Directions to Cook It:

1. Set paddle at the bottom of the bread pan.
2. Add the sour cream to a bread pan and transfer to the Cuisinart Bread Machine
3. Close the lid and select the jam program.
4. Set the timer for 5 minutes to whip the cream until it is fluffy and light.
5. Add the whisked eggs, lemon zest and juice, and vanilla.
6. In a separate bowl, whisk flour, baking soda, and salt.
7. Add flour mix to the whipped cream mixture. Stir.
8. Select the baking option and set the timer for 1 hour
9. When the cake is made, bring it out to cool.

Serving suggestions: CAn be glazed with icing sugar.

Preparation and Cooking Tips: strong white flour can be used in place of all-purpose flour.

Carrot Cake

Carrot cake bread is fruity and delicious. It is usually flavored with cinnamon and brown sugar.

Preparation time: 15 minutes
Cooking time: 60 minutes
Serves: 5

Ingredients To Use:

- 1 ½ cups of all-purpose flour
- 1 tsp of baking powder
- ¾ tsp of baking soda
- 1 tsp of ground cinnamon
- ¼ tsp of salt
- ¼ tsp of ground nutmeg
- 120 ml of canola oil
- 200g of brown sugar
- 1½ cups of shredded carrots

Step-by-Step Directions to Cook It:

1. Set paddle into the bread pan and pour in the flour, baking powder and soda, cinnamon, and nutmeg.
2. In a bowl, add canola oil, eggs, brown sugar, and carrots.
3. Pour the mixture into the bread pan and insert into the Cuisinart Bread Machine
4. Select the bake option and set the timer for 50 minutes.
5. When the cake is ready, bring it out to cool.

Serving suggestions: Serve with creamed cheese.

Preparation and Cooking Tips: add walnuts or pecans, or dried cranberries.

Pumpkin Coffee Cake

Pumpkin coffee cake is sugary, fluffy, and absolutely delectable. It can be enjoyed as breakfast.

Preparation time: 15 minutes

Cooking time: 30 minutes

Serves: 8

Ingredients To Use:

- 250g of all-purpose flour
- 1 tsp of baking soda
- 1 tsp of baking powder
- 1 tsp of ground cinnamon and nutmeg each
- ½ tsp of salt
- 244g pumpkin puree
- 100g brown sugar
- Maple syrup
- 60ml of milk
- 1 tsp Canola oil

Step-by-Step Directions to Cook It:

1. Set paddle into the bread pan and pour in the flour, baking powder and soda, cinnamon, and nutmeg.
2. To a bowl, add the canola oil, milk, brown sugar, and pumpkin puree.
3. Pour the mixture into the bread pan and insert into the Cuisinart Bread Machine
4. Select the bake option and set the timer for 50 minutes.
5. Bring out the cake from the machine and allow cooling.

Serving suggestions: can be glazed with vanilla

Preparation and Cooking Tips: vegetable oil or coconut oil can be used instead of canola

Blueberry Coffee Cake

Blueberry coffee cake is delightful; it is usually served as a quick breakfast with coffee.

Preparation time: 20 minutes

Cooking time: 60minutes

Serves: 10

Ingredients To Use:

- 1 cup of brown sugar
- 1 tsp of ground cinnamon
- 1 cup of all-purpose flour
- ½ cup of butter
- ½ tsp of salt
- ½ cup of milk
- 1 cup of fresh blueberries
- 1 egg
- 1 tsp of vanilla extract

Step-by-Step Directions to Cook It:

1. Whisk egg in a bowl and add sugar, vanilla extract, and milk.
2. In another bowl, mix flour, cinnamon, and baking powder.
3. Add butter and mix with your fingers until the mixture looks like bread crumbs.
4. Remove the paddle from the bread pan and pour in your egg mixture
5. Add the flour mixture.
6. Sprinkle blueberries on the mixture and fix the bread pan into the Cuisinart Bread Machine and cover the lid.
7. Select the start button and choose the bake program, and set the timer for 50minutes.
8. When the cake is ready, bring it out to cool.

Serving suggestions: serve with coffee in the morning

Preparation and Cooking Tips: strong white flour can be used instead of all-purpose flour.

Apple Cinnamon Coffee Cake

Apple cinnamon coffee cake is very nutritious as it is made with fresh apples. It certainly does excite the taste bud.

Preparation time: 20minutes

Cooking time: 45minutes

Serves:10

Ingredients To Use:

- 1 cup of butter
- 1 cup of sugar
- 2/3 brown sugar
- 3 eggs
- 1 tbsp of vanilla
- ¾ cups of sour cream
- 3 cups of flour
- 2 cups of peeled apples

Step-by-Step Directions to Cook It:

1. Set paddle at the bottom of the bread pan, put in your sour cream, put a bread pan in the Cuisinart Bread Machine
2. Close the lid and select the jam program.
3. Set the timer for 5 minutes to whip the cream until it is fluffy and light.
4. Add the whipped cream, whisked eggs, diced apples, butter, sugar, milk, and vanilla.
5. In a separate bowl, whisk the flour, baking soda, and salt. Add it to the whipped cream mixture.
6. Select the baking option and set the timer for 1hour
7. When the cake is ready, bring it out to cool.

Serving suggestions: serve with coffee for breakfast.

Preparation and Cooking Tips: add nuts as toppings; almond, pecans, or walnuts

German Butter Cake

This yummy German butter cake is often served as lunch.

Preparation time: 12 minutes

Cooking time: 25 minutes

Serves: 5

Ingredients To Use:

- 2 teaspoon of active dry yeast
- 1 cup of sugar
- 2 cups of all-purpose flour
- 1 teaspoon of salt
- 1 cup of lukewarm milk

Step-by-Step Directions to Cook It:

1. Set the paddle at the bottom of the bread pan and add milk, sugar, salt, flour, and yeast.
2. Fix bread pan into the Cuisinart Bread Machine machine and cover the lid.
3. Press the start button and select the dough cycle program
4. Set the timer for an hour.
5. Once the knead cycle is over, remove dough from the machine and sprinkle sugar.
6. Put the dough into the machine and select the baking program.
7. Set the timer for 30 minutes.
8. When the cake is ready, bring it out to cool.

Serving suggestions: serve cake when warm

Preparation and Cooking Tips: sprinkle on the dough for a more delicious cake.

CHAPTER 14: WHOLE WHEAT

Cuisinart Whole Wheat Bread

Whole wheat bread is milled from whole wheat grains. It is usually brown and delicious.

Preparation time: 5 minutes

Cooking time: 1hour 15minutes

Serves: 4

Ingredients To Use:

- 283g of tepid water
- 25g of olive oil
- 78g of maple syrup
- White whole wheat flour
- 1 tsp of salt
- 1 tsp of instant yeast

Step-by-Step Directions to Cook It:

1. Pour in your bread pan, tepid water, olive oil, maple syrup, wheat flour, salt, and yeast.
2. Fix bread pan into the Cuisinart Bread Machine and cover the lid.
3. Select the dough program to knead and rise the dough.
4. After the cycle is completed, remove the dough from the bread pan and mold it.
5. Put the molded dough back into the center of the bread pan in the Cuisinart Bread Machine
6. Select the program for whole wheat bread and press the start button.
7. Select medium crust and select 1½ lb loaf size
8. Remove bread from the machine when it is done and allow cooling.

Serving suggestions: eat with jam or butter spread.

Preparation and Cooking Tips: ensure whole wheat is more than the regular bread flour.

Whole Wheat Cinnamon Raisin Bread

Whole wheat cinnamon tasty bread is yummy and delightful. It is fun to eat.

Preparation time: 20 minutes

Cooking time: 60 minutes

Serves: 4

Ingredients To Use:

- 1 cup of warm water
- 1½ cup of whole wheat flour
- 1 tsp of olive oil
- 1 tsp Cinnamon
- 1 tsp Raisin
- 1tsp of yeast

Step-by-Step Directions to Cook It:

1. 1. Pour in your bread pan, tepid water, olive oil, maple, wheat flour, salt, and yeast.
2. Sprinkle raisin all over the mixture
3. Fix bread pan into the Cuisinart Bread Machine and cover the lid.
4. Select the dough program to knead the dough and allow it to go through the Rise cycle.
5. After the dough cycle is completed, bring out the dough from the bread pan and Mold the dough.
6. Put the molded dough back into the center of the bread pan in the Cuisinart Bread Machine
7. Select the program for whole wheat bread program and press the start button.
8. Select medium crust and select 1½ lb loaf size.
9. Remove bread from the machine when it is done and allow cooling.

Serving suggestions: Enjoy plain or as toast.

Preparation and Cooking Tips: in place of raisins, use any dry fruit of your choice.

Whole Wheat Spicy Bread

Whole wheat spicy bread is a unique one. It is delicious and gives an extra spicy taste for you to enjoy.

Preparation time: 3hours

Cooking time: 30minutes

Serves: 3

Ingredients To Use:

- 1 cup of all-purpose flour
- 3 cups of whole wheat flour
- 2 tbsp of active yeast
- 1 tbsp of salt
- 1 tbsp of sugar
- 2 tbsp of melted butter
- 1 cup of tepid water
- 1 tsp of oregano powder
- 1 tsp of chili flakes

Step-by-Step Directions to Cook It:

1. Pour in your bread pan, tepid water, olive oil, chili flakes, oregano powder, wheat flour, salt, and yeast.
2. Fix bread pan into the Cuisinart Bread Machine and cover the lid.
3. Select the dough program to knead the dough and allow it to go through the Rise cycle.
4. After the dough cycle is completed, bring out the dough from the bread pan and Mold the dough.
5. Put the molded dough back into the center of the bread pan in the Cuisinart Bread Machine
6. Select the program for whole wheat bread and press the start button.
7. Select medium crust and select $1\frac{1}{2}$ lb size loaf.
8. Remove bread from the machine when it is done and allow cooling.

Serving suggestions: enjoy it plain with a cup of juice.

Preparation and Cooking Tips: have other types of grounded pepper if you don't desire chili.

Coconut Whole Wheat Bread

Coconut whole wheat bread is delicious, soft, and full of flavor.

Preparation time: 15minutes

Cooking time: 55 minutes

Serves: 5

Ingredients To Use:

- 283g of tepid water
- 25g of olive oil
- 78g of maple syrup
- 2 cups white whole wheat flour
- 1 tsp of salt
- 1 tsp of instant yeast
- 1 cup of coconut milk
- 1 cup of shredded coconut

Step-by-Step Directions to Cook It:

1. Pour tepid water, olive oil, maple syrup, coconut milk, wheat flour (coconut, whole wheat), salt, and yeast into your bread pan.
2. Sprinkle shredded coconut over the mixture.
3. Fix bread pan into the Cuisinart Bread Machine and cover the lid.
4. Select the dough program to knead the dough and allow it to go through the Rise cycle.
5. After the dough cycle is completed, bring out the dough from the bread pan and Mold the dough.
6. Put the molded dough back into the center of the bread pan in the Cuisinart Bread Machine
7. Select the program for whole wheat bread and press the start button.
8. When the bread is done, bring out bread from the machine and let the bread cool.

Preparation and Cooking Tips: use sweet coconut for a better taste

Serving suggestions: eat with a cup of juice

Nutritional value per serving: Calories:345 kcal, Fat:6 g, Carb:65 g, Proteins: 6g

Whole Wheat Mantou

Whole wheat mantou is a Chinese bread recipe. It tastes great.

Preparation time:4 hours

Cooking time: 30 minutes

Serves: 11

Ingredients To Use:

- 2 cups of whole wheat flour
- 1 tsp of active dry yeast
- 1 tbsp of sugar
- 2 cups of all-purpose flour
- 1 tsp of salt
- 1 cup of Tepid water

Step-by-Step Directions to Cook It:

1. Pour in your bread pan, tepid water, wheat flour, salt, and yeast.
2. Fix bread pan into the Cuisinart Bread Machine and cover the lid.
3. Select the dough program to knead the dough and allow it to go through the Rise cycle.
4. After the dough cycle is completed, bring out the dough from the bread pan and Mold the dough.
5. Put the molded dough back into the center of the bread pan in the Cuisinart Bread Machine
6. Select the program for whole wheat bread and press the start button.
7. Select medium crust and select $1\frac{1}{2}$ lb size loaf.
8. Remove bread from the machine when it is done and allow cooling.

Serving suggestions: eat with a drizzle of vegetable oil

Preparation and Cooking Tips: bread flour can be used instead of all-purpose flour.

Nutritional value per serving: Calories: 260kcal, Fat:9 g, Carb:55 g, Proteins:2g

Honey whole wheat bread

Honey whole wheat bread is tasty and a great choice to have as breakfast.

Preparation time: 20 minutes

Cooking time: 55 minutes

Serves: 5

Ingredients To Use:

- 283g of tepid water
- 25g of olive oil
- 1 tsp vinegar
- White whole wheat flour
- 1 tsp of salt
- 1 tsp of instant yeast
- 2 tsp Honey

Step-by-Step Directions to Cook It:

1. Pour tepid water, vinegar, honey wheat flour, salt, and yeast into your bread pan.
2. Fix bread pan into the Cuisinart Bread Machine and cover the lid.
3. Select the dough program to knead the dough and allow it to go through the Rise cycle.
4. After the dough cycle is completed, bring out the dough from the bread pan and Mold the dough.
5. Put the Molded dough back into the center of the bread pan in the Cuisinart Bread Machine
6. Select the program for whole wheat bread and press the start button.
7. Select medium crust and select 1½ lb loaf.
8. Remove bread from the machine when it is ready and allow cooling.

Serving suggestions: serve with tea

Preparation and Cooking Tips: melted butter can be used in place of oil.

Nutritional value per serving: Calories:325 kcal, Fat:3 g, Carb: 58g, Proteins:1g

Tuscan Whole wheat Bread

Tuscan whole wheat bread is a type of herb meal that tastes great and is healthy

Preparation time: 30 minutes

Cooking time: 55 minutes

Serves: 5

Ingredients To Use:

- 283g of tepid water
- 25g of olive oil
- 2 cups of white whole wheat flour
- 1 tsp of salt
- 1 tsp of instant yeast
- 1 tbsp of dried shredded Tuscan leaves

Step-by-Step Directions to Cook It:

1. Pour tepid water, oil, Tuscan leaves, wheat flour, salt, and yeast into your bread pan.
2. Fix bread pan into the Cuisinart Bread Machine and cover the lid.
3. Select the dough program to knead the dough and allow it to go through the Rise cycle.
4. After the dough cycle is completed, bring out the dough from the bread pan and Mold the dough.
5. Put the molded dough back into the center of the bread pan in the Cuisinart Bread Machine
6. Select the program for whole wheat bread and press the start button.
7. Select medium crust and select 1½ lb loaf.
8. Remove bread from the machine when it is ready and allow cooling

Serving suggestions: eat with jam or peanut butter

Preparation and Cooking Tips: melted margarine can be used in place of vegetable oil.

Nutritional value per serving: Calories:300 kcal, Fat: 5g, Carb: 56g, Proteins: 3g

Whole Wheat Rosemary Bread

Whole wheat rosemary bread is yummy and healthy. It can be enjoyed as a sandwich.

Preparation time: 25 minutes

Cooking time: 45 minutes

Serves: 3

Ingredients To Use:

- 283g of tepid water
- 25g of olive oil
- 2 cups of white whole wheat flour
- 1 tsp of salt
- 1 tsp of instant yeast
- 1 tbsp of Shredded Rosemary leaf

Step-by-Step Directions to Cook It:

1. Pour tepid water, oil, rosemary leaf, wheat flour, salt, and yeast into your bread pan.
2. Fix bread pan into the Cuisinart Bread Machine and cover the lid.
3. Select the dough program to knead the dough and allow it to go through the Rise cycle.
4. After the dough cycle is completed, bring out the dough from the bread pan and Mold the dough.
5. Put the molded dough back into the center of the bread pan in the Cuisinart Bread Machine
6. Select the program for whole wheat bread and press the start button.
7. Select medium crust and select 1½ lb loaf size.
8. Remove bread from the machine when it is ready and allow cooling

Serving suggestions: Eat with Strawberry Jam

Preparation and Cooking Tips: strong white flour can be used instead of **bread or** all-purpose flour

Nutritional value per serving: Calories: 245kcal, Fat: 4g, Carb: 55g, Proteins: 2g

APPENDIX : RECIPES INDEX

www.ingramcontent.com/pod-product-compliance
Ingram Content Group UK Ltd.
Pitfield, Milton Keynes, MK11 3LW, UK
UKHW051132260726
13967UKWH00010B/3007

9 781802 443301